To Bonnie and Gregg
In the spirit of Seabrook
Charles H Harrison
4/14/03

Growing a Global Village

Growing a Global Village

Making History at Seabrook Farms

Charles H. Harrison

HM
HOLMES & MEIER
New York / London

Photographs courtesy of the Seabrook Educational and Cultural Center

Published in the United States of America 2003
by Holmes & Meier Publishers, Inc.
160 Broadway • New York, NY 10038
www.holmesandmeier.com

This book has been printed on acid-free paper.

Designed by Brigid McCarthy
Typesetting by JoAnne Todtfeld

Library of Congress Cataloging-in-Publication Data

Harrison, Charles Hampton, 1932–
Growing a global village: Making history at Seabrook Farms / Charles H. Harrison.
p. cm.
Includes bibliographical references and index.
ISBN 0-8419-1428-1 (alk. paper)
1. Seabrook Farms (Seabrook, N.J.)—History. 2. Seabrook (N.J.)—History. 3. Seabrook (N.J.)—Social conditions. 4. Seabrook (N.J.)—Economic conditions. 5. Company towns—New Jersey—Seabrook—History. 6. Minorities—Employment—New Jersey—Seabrook—History. 7. Seabrook, Charles Franklin, 1881–1964. 8. Businessmen—New Jersey—Seabrook—Biography. 9. Seabrook Brothers and Sons—History. 10. Seabrook (N.J.)—Biography. I. Title.

F144.S417H37 2003
974.9'94—dc21

2003040621

Manufactured in the United States of America

Table of Contents

Acknowledgments

After reading the following eight chapters, it will be obvious to the reader that I have relied on—leaned on—many individuals, fifty or more who were kind enough to sit down with me and my tape recorder and tell joyous, sad, exciting, humorous, heart-wrenching, heart-warming, but above all, true stories of how they came to Seabrook Farms, how they fared once they arrived, and, in some cases, what happened to them after they left the global village. Because most of them are identified throughout the book, I shall not list all their names here, but together these people constitute the primary and most helpful source material for the book. I am grateful for the time we shared—and for their offer and my acceptance of an occasional glass of wine or a cup of coffee, and sometimes a slice of German chocolate cake or perhaps a little *mochi* (a delicious Japanese dessert made with rice and pounded red beans).

Special mention must be made of a dozen or so individuals who were especially helpful and, in some cases, indispensable. At the top of the list of indispensables are Ellen Nakamura and John Fuyuume. Ellen was president of the Seabrook Educational and Cultural Center (SECC) when I first became interested in the story of Seabrook Farms and the history-making global village. She was gracious and formal; I doubt she would ever have been comfortable calling me by my first name had we worked together for all these past seven years. Alas, she died before I was able to establish the enduring relationship I desired and most certainly would have cherished. While she was alive, however, she almost always could be found at the Center making sure volunteer workers were doing their assigned tasks and at the same time dispensing knowledge born of experience to all who evidenced genuine interest. I and everyone who ever knew Ellen Nakamura—and that includes governors and ambassadors—miss her.

John Fuyuume bears the title of Project Director, an appellation that is not so much misleading as it is deficient. John, especially since the death of Ellen Nakamura, *is* SECC. He does in fact oversee and handle with care every project that involves SECC, such as this book and a number of smaller publications along with several documentaries about Seabrook Farms (all of which were resources for me). He also lectures and presents slide shows to the groups of children and adults who visit the museum or to those who call on him to travel to their school, college, or organization. He deals enthusiastically with newspaper and television reporters, scholars, and anyone else who wants to learn about the diverse Seabrook population of yesterday that has set such an abiding example for today's American communities. John has been a volunteer since well before the Center officially opened in the fall of 1994, which amounts to more than twelve years of dedicated, unpaid service. It is impossible to remember let alone enumerate all the many ways he has helped me. John, I can truly say, *Arigato gozai mashti* (Thank you so much).

The SECC volunteers, all of whom were invariably kind and helpful, even when I demanded more of them than I probably should have, are Iddy Asada, Chickie Furushima, Terri Masatani, Laye Nagahiro, Sunkie Oye, Helgi Viire and Elaine Yellin.

Thank you all.

Eevi Truumees, Juhan Simonson, and the Reverend Toomas Vaga are all included among the many persons I interviewed and thanked earlier, but each one also assisted me in other ways.

Eevi introduced me to a number of Estonian Americans, including her son, and it was she who asked Jaak Vilms in Colorado to translate for the very first time a portion of his father's wonderful diary that records the terrible ordeal a little band of Estonians endured during their escape from the Red Army, and also recounts the Estonians' early years at Seabrook.

Juhan introduced me to the Estonian library and extensive archives in Lakewood, New Jersey. This treasure house, officially known as the Estonian Archives in the United States, is presided over by the gracious Dr. Olga Berendsen. She kindly allowed me to rummage through boxes of materials that included such items as ships' manifests listing Estonian immigrants who sailed from displaced persons' camps in Germany to ports in the United States. For more than six hundred of those passengers, the journey continued on to Seabrook Farms. The library has an extensive collection of books and other written works pertaining not only to Estonian Americans but also to the larger story of World War II refugees and their attempts to find new life and renewed hope.

After our interview in Lakewood, Reverend Vaga volunteered to drive me into New York City to meet with Maimu Miido, who directed the Estonian Mixed Chorus at Seabrook and who had been well acquainted with C.F. Seabrook.

I met with eighty-six-year-old Jack Seabrook in his office three times and also chatted with him at length by phone. The spacious room where Jack works and meets his guests and the adjacent room of equal size are decorated with pictures and other memorabilia depicting his life and career with Seabrook Farms and some twenty-three other corporations of which he was president, chairman or board member in the forty-plus years after his father sold the company in 1959. Also, here and there, are reminders of the many years that Jack collected and drove historic and elegant horse-drawn carriages. This phase of his life was the subject of a recent book, *Half a Century of Coaching: The Driving Career and Coaches of John M. Seabrook.*

In addition to filling my tapes with the ups and downs and ins and outs of Seabrook Farms, Jack was kind enough to review the first three chapters that had most to do with his father and the business. His corrections and suggested changes were invaluable.

Finally, a special hug for Charlotte Ann, my wife, who never complained when I interrupted her to say, "Let me tell you this wonderful story I heard today" or "Did you know that . . . ," and of course she didn't know "that" because I had just learned about it myself. Then there were the occasions when I had written a sentence or paragraph and it looked and sounded just right and I had to have her read it or listen to it *now,* and not a second later.

Introduction

I grew up in Bergen County in the northeast corner of New Jersey, which today is primarily responsible for the state's not-so-proudly claimed designation as the most urban state of the fifty. When I was young, however, a few small and not very productive truck farms still squeezed themselves in between housing developments. One summer I picked radishes on one of those farms alongside a man who, at the time, seemed ancient to me, and who was well in his cups before arriving for work at 6:00 A.M. But could he pick radishes! He had filled a basket before I could pull and wrap enough bunches to form a short stack next to my aching knees. Alas, all our work—his considerable and mine puny—went for naught, because nearly all the radishes trucked to New York in the morning came back in the afternoon because the farmer couldn't get his price.

I cite this experience not because it gave me any particular knowledge of or appreciation for farming, but because at the time I thought this postage stamp where I worked, and the few remaining others like it in the region, were pretty much what agriculture was like in New Jersey. So this is the Garden State, I thought. Then, many years later, I moved with my family south to Salem County, where I discovered and was astounded by farms that extended as far as the eye could see. So *this* is the Garden State, I now knew. However, what I didn't know at the time was that a good number of those acres and acres and more acres belonged to Seabrook Farms. And it wasn't until seven or eight years ago that I learned that Seabrook Farms at its peak was the greatest frozen food processor in the world and that thousands of men, women, and children displaced and uprooted by war or poverty had made it so.

Introduction

I think that my initial albeit casual awareness of Seabrook Farms occurred when I scanned an article in the local newspaper that reported the fiftieth anniversary celebration of the arrival of 2,500 Japanese Americans at Seabrook Farms beginning in 1944. The article mentioned the Seabrook Educational and Cultural Center on State Highway 77 in Upper Deerfield, and I decided to go to the Center and at least find out what in the world would cause so many Japanese Americans to choose neighboring Cumberland County as a destination after leaving the internment camps out west. The Center is located in the basement of the Upper Deerfield Township Municipal Building, and I wondered, as I clomped down the stairs, whether the long and imposing name of the place might be a deceit. Down in the bowels of the town hall would I find only a tiny, out-of-the-way room with a few artifacts laid out on a dusty table and a single file drawer stuffed full of old, uncataloged clippings and brochures? And there, behind a desk long ago designated surplus by local government, would I be greeted by a very friendly but uninformed lady of advanced years?

Of course, the Center turned out to be quite spacious, encompassing an entire wing of the building, and it was immediately obvious that on the walls, in display cabinets, in dozens of file drawers, on shelves, and in closets were more books, pictures, artifacts, videos and audiotapes, and other memorabilia than I could possibly study in a month, let alone in the hour or so I had allotted for my visit. I was greeted by Ellen Nakamura and John Fuyuume, both of whom not only shared their own experiences and opened up the Center archives to me, but pointed me in all the right directions.

What I learned in that first hour at the Center was that this was not to be a casual encounter; I was up to my journalist's eyeballs in a very important and grand chapter of American history in the twentieth century. Ellen gave me Rei Noguchi's pamphlet about Seabrook Farms, and there in black and white were the astounding statistics: 5,000 workers and their families from twenty-five nations or cultures speaking thirty languages or dialects, working shoulder to shoulder and living side by side in the only rural global village of its kind in the United States; 20,000 or more acres spread over three states, planted with twenty-nine varieties of vegetables and fruits; with 100 million pounds of produce frozen and shipped around the world.

Most of the directions in which Ellen and John pointed me led to people with remarkable stories, each one worthy of public disclosure in a magazine or book or on television. Among them were Japanese American families ripped from their homes and jobs and sent off to internment camps by their own government, Europeans who had dodged bombs and bullets to reach displaced persons camps, out-of-work mountain people who had driven north from Appalachia, much as the Okies had headed west during the Depression, dark-skinned men who had been recruited from the West Indies and spoke with a British accent and preferred cricket to baseball. There are other stories that didn't quite fit the scope of this book and had to be put aside. Perhaps there will be another time and place for them.

Yet I never got to meet Charles F. Seabrook, the man who wrote the opening lines and, in a sense, the closing sentences of this chapter in American history about Seabrook Farms and the men, women and children who peopled the global village. What could he have told me if I had been able to talk with him? What questions would I have asked?

Q. Mr. Seabrook, did you really hate your sons, or did you simply not trust them?

Q. Mr. Seabrook, did you truly have a sense that, in establishing the global village, you were creating a unique experience and experiment in rural America, or were you simply proud that you had found sources of cheap and grateful labor?

Q. Mr. Seabrook, what can you tell me about those years from 1913 to 1964 that no one else can tell, because no one else knows?

Hanging on one wall in the office at the Seabrook Educational and Cultural Center is a weathered board that was found a few years ago in a falling-down shed near the small farm operated by C. F. and his father at the turn of the twentieth century. Chiseled into the board is the name "Charles F. Seabrook." Do you suppose he could have imagined then as a youth that his name would be identified with one of the great achievements in American business—the successful merger of agriculture and industry—and with the creation of rural America's first and only grand experiment in communal living?

Growing a Global Village

Chapter 1

Transplanting Uprooted Peoples

In the first half of the twentieth century, in provincial Cumberland County, New Jersey, 125 miles south of New York City but closer to Old Dixie's heart and soul, a seed planted by a father and son grew into the first and only rural global village of its kind in America. The thousands of men, women, and children who worked and lived there from 1900 to 1960 represented three races and twenty-five national origins or cultures; they spoke thirty languages or dialects. Most came with empty pockets and empty dreams, but they also came with hope.

The place was called Seabrook Farms.

In 1908, Israel Zangwill, who grew up in a Jewish ghetto in London, wrote *The Melting Pot,* a play in which he portrayed

Europeans crossing the Atlantic to melt and reform in "God's crucible"—America. It was always assumed that our largest cities, New York, Chicago, and Philadelphia, would be the melting pots, and so they were.

Tides of immigrants rolled into our metropolitan areas and created enclaves such as Little Italy, Chinatown, and Spanish Harlem. To be sure, some immigrants moved into the countryside. For example, a number of Germans, including some Hessian soldiers who had been captured or had deserted the British ranks during the American Revolution, settled in Lancaster County, Pennsylvania, and Swedish families became farmers in Wisconsin. However, only at Seabrook Farms, in all of the United States, did the melting pot, in such gigantic proportions, move out of the cities.

This first of America's agri-industries, which pioneered frozen foods and was the provisioner of the United States armed forces and most of the free world during World War II, brought to this piece of flat and sandy soil men and women who needed a home, a job, and a future. Early on they were White Russian soldiers escaping the Bolshevik Revolution and Italians direct from the mother country or by way of Pennsylvania's coal mines. In the early years of World War II, hundreds of men arrived by boat and train from the islands of the West Indies. At the end of the war 2,500 Japanese Americans left the internment camps in the west, where they had been confined by their own government, and headed east to Seabrook Farms instead of returning to the small farms and businesses that had been stolen from them in California. Shortly thereafter, hundreds of families from nearly every country in Europe made their way to Seabrook Farms, many growing silent and prayerful as the troop ships that brought them to our shores along with homecoming GIs sailed past the Statue of Liberty. It was at Seabrook Farms that these people joined African Americans from the Deep South and country folk from Appalachia, many of whom arrived in third-hand jalopies and broken-down pickups piled high with every stick of furniture and piece of clothing they owned, which wasn't much.

This truly global village was no Camelot—the people worked hard, long hours—but it will never be forgotten, because American history was written here.

Transplanting Uprooted Peoples

Charles Franklin Seabrook, who was most responsible for finding jobs for all these people and for growing the global village to accommodate them, and whose postage-stamp truck farm just north of Bridgeton mushroomed into the "biggest vegetable factory on earth," hated farming. John Seabrook, writing in the *New Yorker,* said of his grandfather: "As a farmer, C. F. was distinguished by a strong dislike of dirt."[1] Jack Seabrook, father of John and youngest of C. F.'s three sons, called his father a man of "incredible contradictions." He was beloved by thousands of uprooted and destitute men and women to whom he gave home, work, and a future, but he never had a close friend. Perhaps contradictions were in the Seabrook genes. Distant ancestor Marion Seabrook and his immediate heirs were slaveholding plantation owners in South Carolina, while C. F.'s grandfather Samuel worked for the abolitionist newspaper editor Horace Greeley.[2]

C. F.—only the bold and the brave and his wife, Norma, called him Charlie—was a short, thin man, austere behind his spectacles even when he was smiling. He began his love-hate relationship with farming when, at age twelve in 1893, he quit school to work full-time weeding onions on his father's truck farm in what is now Upper Deerfield.[3] The 1923 *Who's Who in New Jersey* noted that C. F. "never selected a profession. He just naturally grew up as a farmer, doing for his father the work of an ordinary farmhand." He told the story of how he once broke his leg and his father insisted he accompany him in the horse and wagon to deliver that day's produce. His father at least cushioned the ride with a pillow.[4] C. F. later said to Bruce Barton, an interviewer for the *American Magazine* (May 1921) that "people who write poems to farming never got up before dawn to milk cows seven days a week and never weeded onions on their knees in the heat and mosquitoes."[5]

Perhaps what finally convinced C. F. that he could overcome his aversion to dirt and weeds was his realization early on that agriculture and industry could be successfully and profitably combined. The likely turning point occurred at age fourteen when he learned of a Danish farmer who had found a way to keep his crops from shriveling during dry spells by stretching iron pipes with holes over his fields and forcing water through them. F. Alan Palmer, who once worked for Seabrook Farms and then wrote a book about Upper Deerfield, described what happened next: "As an experiment, C. F. installed a line of pipe over a bed of celery plants. The test was such a success that in due time [by 1920] Seabrook Farms not only had the distinction of being the first commercial growing enterprise where overhead irrigation was installed on a large scale, but remained the largest single such installation in the world with more than 250 acres devoted to intensive vegetable growing. It has been estimated that the average increase in crop returns where such irrigation was used was from two to three hundred percent."[6]

C. F. divulged his true heart's desire for a career in the 1921 interview in the *American Magazine:* "All my life, I wanted to be a construction engineer."[7] By 1913, his wish had come true. Seabrook Farms was incorporated that year, and, as a result, the company attracted working capital, primarily from New York investors W. A. and A. M. White and Edgar L. Smith. With cash in the bank and a certificate from a correspondence school of engineering in his pocket, C. F. formed his own construction business, first calling it the C. F. Seabrook Company and later the Seabrook Engineering Corporation. He owned the business totally.[8] It was not connected legally or financially to Seabrook Farms, except that C. F. of Seabrook Farms could hire C. F. of Seabrook Engineering Corporation to build "this and that," and C. F., the self-taught and self-employed construction engineer, proceeded to build a lot of this and that.

His list of accomplishments during the next eight years might astound any twenty-first-century contractor. He built thirty-five miles of roads, including most of modern State Highway 77 that connects Bridgeton with the northern counties and, not incidentally, was at the time a conduit for Seabrook trucks moving products to markets in Philadelphia, New York, and elsewhere. At Seabrook Farms Central, located on Parsonage Road between Route 77 and the Bridgeton-Deerfield Pike in Upper Deerfield Township, he constructed power and food-processing plants, a cold storage warehouse, several shops, a sawmill, dams for water storage and the pipelines and pumping stations to supply the vast irrigation system he had designed, houses for an increasing number of employees, and two railroad connections. One track hooked up to the Pennsylvania Railroad and the other to the Central of

New Jersey line. C. F. figured the two systems could battle for Seabrook Farms business, thereby guaranteeing his company the best rate.[9]

Perhaps his crowning achievement at the time—and it was both a political and a professional coup—was the construction of a consolidated school for grades one through eight, one of the first of its kind in bucolic South Jersey. At the time, students in the area had been attending a scattering of one-, two-, and three-room schools. However, before C. F. could erect his school, he had to pull some important strings tied to state legislators who looked with favor on his company, which was fast becoming a major employer in New Jersey. To his advantage, C. F. was a member of the State Highway Commission, an appointment that recognized his ability to build good roads. In 1920 the people of Deerfield Township voted against C. F.'s proposed consolidated school. Two years later he persuaded the legislature to pass a bill authorizing a referendum to be held in Deerfield Township that would, if voters approved, result in breaking off the northern-most piece of the old township (incorporated in 1748) to create Upper Deerfield Township. On the day of the referendum, April 3, 1922, the vote was 254 for the new municipality and 65 against. "Considering the season of the year, with practically every farmer in the fields, yesterday's vote may be considered both reasonably heavy and decisive," the *Bridgeton Evening News* reported.[10]

Unfortunately, C. F.'s building binge outran his investors' money, so they fired him and sold the business to Del-Bay Farms in 1924. C. F. regained control in October 1929 by forming a new group of investors. Of course, at the end of that month the stock market crashed and the country slipped into the Great Depression. Characteristically, however, C. F. was upbeat about the future, although he admitted that others might have reason to be less enthusiastic. "There has always been a great difference of opinion among both bankers and economists as to whether or not agricultural production could be industrialized to an extent at all comparable to that achieved in manufacturing."[11] Always up to a challenge, no matter how daunting, C. F. set out to prove he could and would revolutionize farming by turning it into an industry—

at the time, in the early 1930s, not even a dream, let alone a plan of action, among American farmers.

By the start of World War II, Seabrook Farms had become the first agri-industry in the world. B. C. Forbes, founder of *Forbes* magazine, labeled C. F. the "Henry Ford of Agriculture,"[12] and *Reader's Digest,* in January 1944, reprinted an article from *Coronet* magazine that called C. F. the world's first assembly-line farmer. "Seabrook Farms, in the flat, sandy stretches of southern New Jersey are probably the most highly mechanized farms in the country," wrote Mona Gardner in the *Coronet* article. Seabrook "has built a vast dehydrating and canning plant, and a freezing plant which is the largest in the world."[13]

The alliance of C. F. to Clarence Birdseye, the frozen food maven, was a partnership of forward-thinking, deal-making risk-takers. Courtney Seabrook, C. F.'s middle son, recalled how Birdseye had journeyed to Labrador in 1912 and again in 1916 as, of all things, a fur trader. There he lived with an Eskimo family and assisted the man of the igloo in hoisting heavy poles joined by a line that could support the weight of seal, fish, and other animal carcasses whose meat would feed the family for months. The practice of preserving fresh food by freezing it was not lost on the thirty-year-old Birdseye.

A decade after his trip to the north country, Birdseye began experiments in his Massachusetts laboratory designed to come up with a way to freeze fish by means other than hanging it outdoors from a stretched fishing line in below-zero weather. In 1929, Belford Seabrook, C. F.'s oldest son, who had heard of Birdseye's work, visited the fur-trader-turned-inventor in his laboratory. Belford had just completed his freshman year at Princeton University in pursuit of a degree in civil engineering (C. F. had decreed that his two oldest sons would be engineers, not farmers).

The following summer, with his father's encouragement, Belford tried to duplicate Birdseye's experimentation, using ammonia from the ice plant C. F. had built during World War I to cool railroad freight cars. On the basis of Belford's mostly successful tinkering, C. F. had his long-time chauffeur, Jonas McGalliard, drive him up to New York City and the offices of the General Foods Corporation at 250 Park Avenue. General Foods had purchased the Birdseye patent for quick-freezing food in retail packages. C. F. persuaded General Foods that Seabrook Farms had the land, equipment, and know-how to plant, pick, and freeze more than fish—a lot more—and, of course, C. F. assured General Foods that the packages shipped to stores would carry the Birdseye label. The Birdseye brand dominated the frozen food market for many years thereafter, and it made Seabrook "the brightest spot in the economy of southern New Jersey." Later, Seabrook produced frozen food under its own label.[14]

In the mid-1920s, historian Alfred M. Heston referred to C. F. as "foremost among the agriculturists of the United States."[15] By the mid-1930s, C. F. was fast becoming foremost among agri-industrialists. But who was the real person behind the hugely resourceful and successful industrialized farmer who abhorred getting his hands dirty in soil but didn't mind the grease and grime associated with building roads, bridges, and food-processing plants?

The simple answer is that no one ever became fully acquainted with the man inside the man, neither his family nor the men and women who respectfully and affectionately referred to him as the Old Man and remain forever grateful that he brought them into his global village and gave them new lives. However, two elemental truths about C. F. have emerged from what family members and employees have said about him, either in conversation or in their writing. The first is that C. F. genuinely liked people, as long as they never tried to crack the shell that protected his true self. The second is that he enjoyed life more as an observer than a participant. One gets the distinct impression, for example, that, for C. F., having a really good time was watching others having a really good time.

In light of the first truth, what can we say about this grower of the global village? Was he a humanitarian devoted to the promotion of human welfare, or was he simply a good businessman who hired, rather cheaply, mostly people who came to his village with not much more than one change of clothes and a pocketful of coins and who, after all, had nowhere else to go?

C. F. didn't do what he did for humanitarian reasons, said son Jack flat out. "If you had asked him if he was a humanitarian, he probably would have been upset and responded, 'Hey, I'm no pinko.'" Jack seemed to be saying that his father, a true-blue conservative from his panama hat to his wing-tipped shoes, would have considered humanitarianism—aiding the downtrodden on the basis of philanthropic principle—as some sort of left-leaning humbug. "It was fun for him," Jack said matter-of-factly. For example, Jack continued, his father flew to Europe in 1952 to sponsor more families displaced by war, not out of goodheartedness, but because he wanted to travel overseas one last time even if it wasn't aboard a transatlantic luxury ship as he had done in the 1920s with his engineering firm. Furthermore, Jack went on, the addition of hundreds of workers recruited from the displaced persons camps meant that Seabrook Farms would have to put up more housing to accommodate them, and, of course, C. F. took great pleasure in building something.

Jack's rather cynical point of view is based, in part, on a contentious family history, as noted later in this chapter, but perhaps it also emanates from his deep-seated hurt that Seabrook's employees often misdirected their praise and thanks. He cites, for example, that it was he and his brothers, not C. F., who were ultimately responsible for recruiting the majority of workers in the 1940s and 1950s and seeing to their needs. At the fiftieth anniversary event celebrating the arrival of the first wave of Japanese Americans from the internment camps, Jack said, people were singing the praises of C. F. He, brother Courtney, and brother Belford's sons were all in the audience, and they were well aware that when some people lauded what Mr. Seabrook had done, the Mr. Seabrook they were referring to was more likely one of the sons rather than the father. In an interview, Jack Seabrook illustrated what he meant: "There is a marvelous scene [in the videotape shown at the occasion] where Samah Pearson [a leader among the Jamaican workers] talks about going into the office of Mr. Seabrook because his door was always open. Well, that was my office, but everybody listening thought it was C. F.'s office."

If you were to confront any one of the dwindling number of Seabrook Farms alumni—workers and their bosses—still living in the Bridgeton area or scattered throughout the country and ask them whether C. F. was a humanitarian, almost all would reply in the affirmative. The majority of them address the question in the same way they came to Seabrook: without baggage; in this case, without having experienced the bitterness and alienation within the family that may have colored Jack Seabrook's appraisal of his father's feelings and motives.

Most of the men and women who came to work at Seabrook Farms in the period from 1930 to 1960 are deceased, but their children, many of whom are a few years either side of age seventy, recall the generosity they attribute to C. F. For them it starts with their parents' recruitment or sponsorship. Japanese Americans credit the Old Man with the plan to bring them east from the despair of internment camps to the promise of a job and hope for the future. Europeans escaping the devastation and terror of World War II and its aftermath would find it nearly impossible to believe Jack's explanation of why his father went to Germany in 1952. Because C. F. liked to travel? Certainly not! And when families arrived at Seabrook with their few belongings and empty pockets, who assured them that they could eat free at the company cafeteria and shop free at the company store for up to six months? Didn't that assurance come directly from C. F.? When interviewed in 1996 and asked for her impression of C. F., the late Ellen Nakamura, who was among the very first Japanese Americans to arrive from the camps in 1944, said, "Mr. Seabrook, to most of us who have remained [in the area] over the years and more than likely to many others who left, was a very, very wonderful person—brilliant, generous and kind."

Somewhere in between Jack Seabrook's cynical view and Mrs. Nakamura's gushing is John Melchiorre's assessment of C. F.: "Was he a humanitarian? Absolutely. He was truly interested in people and their welfare. I think he was proud of being able to offer jobs to [those who were misplaced or displaced] and to give them a start." Melchiorre's view has to be given credence. For twenty years, from 1950 to 1970, he was personnel manager and saw C. F. almost daily for much of that period.

In basic agreement with Melchiorre is Endel Miido, who escaped the Soviet invasion of Estonia in 1944 and arrived in the United States in 1949 from a displaced persons camp in Germany. Shortly after coming to work at Seabrook Farms, Miido was unexpectedly plucked by C. F. from his job on the loading dock of the cold storage plant and given two white-collar positions: assistant paymaster and, more important, assistant to the president—C. F. himself—for a department called Displaced Persons Affairs. In the latter role, Miido, who was C. F.'s junior by forty years, first traveled to Washington with the Old Man to visit the offices of the Displaced Persons Commission established by the 1948 Displaced Persons Act and then accompanied C. F. on the flight to Germany referred to by Jack Seabrook. Although Jack implies that the men recruited by his father in Germany in the early 1950s were not really needed then as employees of Seabrook Farms (the company began laying off workers in 1953), Miido disagrees. C. F. went there with a list of skilled workers he was particularly looking to hire, such as carpenters, electricians and others.

The displaced persons who came to Seabrook in the period 1949 to 1953 are probably most thankful to C. F. because of the meetings he periodically scheduled with them to hear their gripes and requests concerning anything and everything: housing, working conditions, hours, pay, their children's teachers, what they thought was missing on the shelves of the company store, and so on. C. F. was a generous person, Miido said. He cited C. F.'s largesse on behalf of the Estonian folk choir (he loved music, particularly singing): season tickets to choir members for performances at the Philadelphia Opera House. One of C. F.'s most generous acts was to offer Miido and his family the opportunity to rent, at low cost, a house down Polk Lane from the Seabrook estate in Upper Deerfield. As neighbors, the Miidos spent more time with the Seabrooks than most other workers. An added perk was unlimited access to C. F.'s in-ground pool (also occasionally opened to members of the Estonian folk choir and the local Girl Scouts).

It was not uncommon for C. F. to drop in at workers' homes unannounced. Often, the reason for the visit was to satisfy his appetite for a favorite dish concocted by the family. Clara Clark Holt, who came with her parents to Seabrook from eastern Tennessee in 1940 at age three, remembers in the 1950s C. F. stopping by for her mother's Appalachian-style apple pie and a cup of coffee. The Old Man took a particular liking to Estonian raisin bread—or was it the vodka with which he washed it down? He would knock once on the door to Albert Vilms's prefab house on Second Street, enter, and then ask, "Do you have any raisin bread?" According to Eevi Truumees, Estonian raisin bread, called *kringel,* is a richer, fuller-bodied version of supermarket raisin bread most Americans are accustomed to, and the dough containing the raisins is twisted like a pretzel before baking.

But the Old Man's visits were not always social. Sometimes he came around because he genuinely wanted to help solve a problem or satisfy a need, particularly when the problem or need was associated with work or company housing. When Seabrook Farms decided to erect a number of prefabricated homes on slabs at the northwest corner of Parsonage Road and Route 77 to accommodate the expanding workforce, it was first necessary to move a house already sitting on the lot. The house, also owned by the company, was occupied at the time by Clara Clark's family, consisting of mother and father, six children, and an expected new baby. Clara Clark Holt recalled that it was still winter when the house was moved across the street and set on blocks temporarily. Unfortunately, the temporariness extended past the birth of the child, and the baby, nursing mother, and just about all the other children came down with a nasty virus as a consequence of the cold wind swirling around the foundationless dwelling. Word of the situation at the Clark house reached the Old Man and he showed up at the house to promise prompt relief. Shortly thereafter a crew arrived on the scene to construct a foundation.

Most of the men and women who came to work at Seabrook Farms during the first half of the twentieth century were thankful for the work and the benefits of living in a company town. However, the respect accorded the Old Man by the Europeans and the Japanese Americans (primarily the issei, who had been born and raised in Japan) was special, mainly because of their upbringing. Helgi Malleus Viire, an Estonian, recalls her first day at Seabrook School. When the teacher entered the room, Helgi immediately jumped to her feet, much to the surprise and snickering of the other children. And it was not uncommon for issei to bow upon meeting for the first time a neighbor from the next housing unit.

It does not seem to be a contradiction that those who held C. F. in high esteem also acknowledged that the Old Man profited greatly by hiring people who, because of their straits, would work very hard for very little money. The late Renford Glanville, a Jamaican, told about a time when a group of fellow Jamaicans coming off the night shift went to a local Bridgeton diner for breakfast. The owner refused to serve them because of their color. As a result, according to Glanville, the men "turned the whole place upside down." Then, someone—it isn't clear whether it was one of the workers or the diner's owner—got on the phone to "Mr. Seabrook," who told the owner to give the men whatever they wanted. Glanville concluded the story by implying that Mr. Seabrook issued his order to the diner's owner not because of a special concern for the workers' welfare or to protest racial discrimination, but "because we were making that man money, believe me."[16] In truth, the Mr. Seabrook who gave the order was Jack.

The late F. Alan Palmer, a longtime Seabrook employee, called C. F. a just and fair employer, "in a way, that is." The "way" was to pay workers however much it took to satisfy them, nothing more. For most of the men and women who came to work at Seabrook Farms in the first half of the twentieth century, it didn't take much. After all, they came with nothing and had few, if any, other job prospects at the time. On one occasion, C. F. learned that an employee "in a relatively important niche was stealing equipment regularly. [C. F.] replied that he was fully aware of it and that the value of the purloined material amounted to a certain sum each month; that amount, combined with the salary the man received, came to what he was actually worth as an employee." Palmer's appraisal of C. F. as employer concluded with this observation: "There is no question but that C. F. had a paternalistic attitude toward 'his' people; he was always ready to lend assistance to those whom he considered worthy of the expenditure of effort. At the same time he could be mighty cold toward anyone who attempted to use him."[17]

In his little book about C. F. and the history of Seabrook Farms, *The Henry Ford of Agriculture,* which is an extension of the text of a long speech he delivered on the occasion of the fiftieth anniversary of the arrival of Japanese Americans, Jack Seabrook shared some of the family history that painted a different picture of C. F. "Until I was thirteen years old in 1930," he spoke and wrote, "I hardly knew my father at all. Even if he was at home, he was not the sort of father who paid any attention to small children, and after I was seven, in 1924, I saw him only on his occasional visits to South Jersey and had little contact with him." At the time, C. F. was heavily engaged in his engineering-construction business and spent most of his days and nights either in New York City or overseas. Later in the 1930s, Jack was assigned by his father to work in the cannery laboratory grading vegetables.

> C. F. was probably pleased with my laboratory work, but I never remember his visiting it or saying he was pleased. The nearest he ever came was to tell people, often in my presence, "Jack is an example of the fact that, as time goes on, generations get weaker but wiser." This was a reference to the fact that I was tall and very thin in my teens and certainly not the physical specimen that Belford, a high school athlete, was. Anyhow, I took it as the nearest thing to a compliment I was ever going to get.
>
> Seen up close, as we saw him, C. F. was cold and distant, but, in public, he was highly successful at projecting a warm, caring, friendly image to a large group that would never get in close. Once in a great while at a gala family party, C. F. would project a warmer image to the grandchildren, but, at most family parties, there was tension, because C. F. was being cruelly and sarcastically critical of some family member, a daughter-in-law who was hard of hearing or a pre-teen grandson who happened to be overweight. The food and drink at these parties were magnificent and abundant, but attendance by the family was compulsory.[18]

The second elemental truth—that C. F.'s idea of a good time was watching others having a good time—probably follows from the first, as Jack expressed it. He may have been at his happiest, at least when he was at home in Upper Deerfield, when he staged a big party at which a large number of people would gather for fine food and drink (C. F.'s stock of wine and liquor was probably the largest and most selective of any in southern New Jersey). He was always cordial to his guests, but on these occasions he might stand apart and merely observe them as they ate, imbibed, laughed, and danced.

The grandest parties of all were those scheduled for New Year's Eve, when a lighted sign over the driveway wished guests the glad tidings of the night. To these parties, C. F. invited everybody who was anybody in local, state and federal politics (or at least those Republican politicians who recognized Seabrook Farms as a major employer in the region and knew C. F. as an influential force in the New Jersey GOP). Also on hand were Hollywood celebrities, not in great numbers but of great popularity at the time, such as Eva Gabor. In the midst of all that glittered was C. F., in formal dress and glass in hand, the sun about which the evening's fun and frolickers revolved—but at a distance. He preferred it that way, and those in the sun's orbit knew how close they could get before the radiated warmth might suddenly cool. Nothing gave him greater pleasure in the late 1940s and early 1950s than to show off the Estonian singers and dancers at his parties. "He enjoyed us tremendously," said Eevi Truumees, one of the singers, "but it was as though he was always looking in at us."

Humanitarian and hard-nosed businessman; especially warm to those workers who returned his warmth respectfully and gratefully and cool to many people who were his equals or who knew him too well, including and especially his family; fond of merriment but not a man to make merry—C. F. was all of these, truly a man of contradictions. Arguably the greatest agri-industrialist of his time and unquestionably the planter and cultivator of rural America's only global village, he unfortunately saved the granddaddy of contradictions to reveal toward the end of his life, and its consequences were devastating. With one swipe of his pen he effectively destroyed all that he and others had so carefully built up over fifty-plus years.

Beginning in 1913, when he took over the truck farm from his father, C. F. was a driven man. He attended to business most of his waking hours, and his waking hours often included nights as well as days. "Apparently requiring little sleep, Mr. Seabrook was never happier than during the times of the year when there was twenty-four hour harvesting of crops and the processing of vegetables. He would walk up to some sleepy individual working on the packing line at three A.M. and, addressing him or her by name, would enter into a conversation concerning a matter of presumed mutual interest—naturally usually pertaining to the job being performed and often including a suggestion of how the work might be done more efficiently." Then, before dawn, he might get someone to drive him out to the fields, where again he would talk to workers.[19]

By the 1950s, however, the strain of all those years of hard driving and the lingering aftereffects of an undiagnosed illness in 1941—probably a stroke—were taking their toll. C. F. had lost much of the confidence he had shown in the decades when he alone was making all the major decisions and most of the minor ones. Very reluctantly, and not with grace or with much appreciation for their efforts, he relinquished his firm grip on day-to-day operations, and his sons—the "boys," as he called them—assumed control over the business and the global village.

Some have called the global village that sprouted under the guidance of the Old Man and was later nourished by his sons a microcosm of the United Nations. That may be so, but it also represented in a small way and, of course, over a far briefer period, the history of our nation, our democracy. The eminent historian Henry Steele Commager, in a conversation with Bill Moyers, said "the miracle" of the United States is "that the democratic system worked." In the beginning, he continued, there was scant reason to think it would prosper. The seemingly insurmountable problem—not then or now faced to the same degree by any other nation in the world—was to get widely diverse peoples to live in relative harmony. The difficulty, Commager said, was "to get . . . cohesion in a country of so many races and so many languages and so many religions and so many backgrounds of one kind or another."[20]

Fortunately—and miraculously, if Commager is to be believed—both America and the global village at Seabrook Farms found a way to "get cohesion." Rei R. Noguchi came to Seabrook Farms with his parents from a World War II internment camp. He is now a professor of English at California State University. In 1994 he wrote *Seabrook: A New Beginning,* a pamphlet that commemorated the fiftieth anniversary of the arrival of the first Japanese American families at Seabrook Farms. In his introduction, Noguchi refers to the "global bootstrap village, where downtrodden yet hardy peoples of diverse cultures were given a chance to regenerate their lives. Uprooted by powerful national and international . . . events . . . most of Seabrook's settlers and workers arrived as displaced peoples. Whatever their origin, these diverse, uprooted peoples encountered an unfamiliar but receptive soil in Seabrook. Although some left after only a few years, many decided to stay. Here they planted their seeds, and their severed lives again took root."[21]

C. F. died on October 20, 1964, the same day former president Herbert Hoover died. In an editorial two days later, the *Bridgeton Evening News* called C. F. "a man of special vision, one who looked ahead and caught the spirit of American progress during one of its greatest eras of achievement."[22] His vision was more than fulfilled by the great agri-industry that bore his name and by a multicultural workforce never before or since equaled in America. The chapters that follow constitute the story of that workforce—often desperate and destitute men and women and their families, who came from many corners of this land and from lands far away and found in a small patch of southern New Jersey a job, a home, and—most important of all—a future.

Chapter 2

"No Sulkers Need Apply"

On a cold Saturday three days into the new year of 1913, Arthur P. Seabrook loaded his wagon with produce for his last delivery to customers in Bridgeton. An article in the *Dollar Weekly News* of January 24, 1913 recorded that the new owners of the little truck farm Mr. Seabrook had tilled since 1886 had already purchased another sixty-eight acres, bringing the total acreage of the farm near the intersection of Beebe Run and Seeley Lake Roads in Hopewell Township up to about one hundred and twenty-five.[1] The article never mentioned that the new owner was none other than Arthur's son, Charles Franklin—known to nearly everyone as C. F.—now incorporated and trading as Seabrook Farms Company.

C. F. and A. P. (his father also was known familiarly by his initials) had been contentious partners in the business of growing and selling premium quality vegetables locally and to markets in New York, Philadelphia, and Baltimore. They frequently disagreed on how aggressive they and the business should be. A. P. was basically content to grow the very best vegetables, make a decent living, expand slowly if at all, and retire to a nice but unpretentious house in nearby Bridgeton before he got too old to farm. C. F., from the day he first worked as a farmhand, had his sights set on making the truck farm into an agri-business—big, mechanized, and prosperous. He gave no thought to retirement, but he did plan on getting out of the fields and into a management office at the first opportunity.

Fifty-one years from the time when C. F. bought out his father and A. P. Seabrook and Son became Seabrook Farms, the *Bridgeton Evening News* placed this quotation from British Prime Minister James Ramsay MacDonald above C. F.'s obituary: "Nobody has ever established a successful business without dreaming about it in the beginning."[2] It is unlikely that C. F. ever read or heard the statement, but he lived as though he had memorized it at an early age.

C. F. wasted no time in making his dreams—the bigger, the better—come true. Whereas A. P. would have been content to expand by using profits from the business, C. F. realized immediately that the kind of growth he was dreaming about required outside capital, and lots of it. He bought his father's share of the business and sold it at a considerable profit to the wealthy White family, who then became an equal partner. The deal allowed Seabrook Farms, by the end of 1913, to purchase a number of small farms in what was then Deerfield Township (now Upper Deerfield) and thereby add another 200 acres, to double the acreage irrigated by overhead pipes, build a greenhouse 300 feet long and sixty feet wide, and open nine new boarding houses for an expanding workforce of single men who came primarily from Philadelphia and the surrounding area. Although he was unschooled and untrained in civil engineering, C. F. formed his own construction business with the White money and commenced a rapid buildup of the company's infrastructure.[3]

As early as 1914, the permanent workforce lived and worked in homely dormitories in what amounted to a company town. In later years, the company town grew into a global village—actually a collection of little villages—housing men, women, and families of many nationalities and speaking many languages, but it always was a company town. It just got bigger. In 1913, and at least for the rest of that decade, single men only were wanted. Wives and children were tolerated in the 1920s and 1930s, but, by the 1940s families were actively recruited. The reason for the change in hiring practices was the change in the nature of the business and the volume of output. For example, women tolerated the tedium of sorting vegetables on an assembly line much better than men.

Single men were preferred in the early years simply because it was easier to feed and house them. Like the army, the company could stack bunks in rows and provide one gang latrine and bathhouse instead of two. And although the company might be more conscious of the kinds of meals that were served to women and children and how those meals were served, it concluded—as an army mess sergeant might—that men were more likely to accept the plainest food dished out quickly and none too graciously.

Very little recruitment took place in the early years of Seabrook Farms. Most men who came looking for work had heard about job opportunities by word of mouth. For example, Italian immigrants who arrived at Seabrook in the years before World War I had heard about Seabrook Farms either from relatives already in the area, particularly in the Italian neighborhoods of south Philadelphia, or from immigration agents at the port of Gloucester City. At that time, Gloucester City, across the Delaware River from Philadelphia and downriver from Camden, was one of the busier ports of entry that together processed nearly six million immigrants who entered America between 1911 and 1920.

From the mid-nineteenth century until 1930, Italy was a country of mass emigration, most of it to the United States. In 1913 alone, the year C. F. created Seabrook Farms, 565,000 Italians emigrated to this country. The migration was fueled by periodic economic crises, particularly in southern Italy, and political unrest. A number of Italian men left their native land in the half-dozen or so years before the outbreak of World War I to avoid fighting in the Italo-Turkish War of 1911–12, during which Italy occupied Libya, and because they saw new war clouds gathering after Austria endangered the Triple Alliance by occupying Bosnia. Many of those men had worked on farms in their homeland.[4]

The United States may not have been ready for World War I, but Seabrook Farms was. Because of its tremendous expansion since 1913, by the time America got into the war in 1917 Seabrook Farms was prepared to supply our armed forces and free peoples everywhere with fresh and canned fruits and vegetables: lima beans, spinach, beets, pumpkins and squash, lettuce, celery, tomatoes, peppers, cabbages, potatoes, turnips, leeks, rhubarb, and strawberries. The great demand for food enabled Seabrook Farms to up its prices, so wartime became a very profitable time for the company. With some of the profits, C. F. planted eleven varieties of peach trees and twelve varieties of apple trees on hundreds of new acres.

As the war was winding down, a number of the single Italian men working at Seabrook Farms set sail for Italy, only to return shortly thereafter with a wife and sometimes a child or two. Other workers married daughters of Italian families who had settled in south Philadelphia. Then, in the early 1920s, still more Italian immigrant men and their families arrived at Seabrook. Many were escapees from the Pennsylvania coal mines. The mines had been a prime attraction for immigrants arriving in the ports of Philadelphia and Gloucester City until the hard, punishing hours underground took their toll on the men, most of whom were accustomed to working outdoors in the fields and vineyards of the old country.

Because of the addition of women and children, C. F.—always happy to be building something—constructed rows of neat little houses that soon came to be called the Italian Village. This enclave was the nucleus of what would become, in the 1940s and 1950s, the great global village that holds such a special place in the long history of creating America and Americans from the peoples of the wide world.

Among those who arrived in Seabrook at the beginning of the 1920s was the Chiari family, whose story is different from that of almost every other Italian family who came during that period: the wife got to Seabrook first. Giovanni Chiari entered the United

States through Ellis Island and found work in a coal mine north of Altoona, Pennsylvania. Like so many other single Italian men, he returned to Italy to find a wife. Giovanni stayed long enough with his bride in a small town twenty miles outside Rome to father four children, who accompanied their parents to America sometime after World War I.

Even before he left the coal pits to go back to Italy, Giovanni's health had been affected by the damp and cold of the mines. At some point between 1920 and 1925—no descendants are quite sure of the precise date—Giovanni's wife, Dominica, decided that none of the children would follow in their father's footsteps coming home at night blackened and wheezing from coal dust. She heard that the orchards near Hammonton, New Jersey, were hiring, so that summer she took the children and went off to pick peaches. She soon learned that Seabrook Farms down in Cumberland County was paying more to field hands. Dominica and the children traveled to Seabrook, where they spent the summer gathering beans. Mother and children, now numbering nine, returned to Seabrook the following summer and stayed until the end of the growing season. Back home with Giovanni, she issued an ultimatum: Next year the family is going to Seabrook for good. Then the inevitable question: Are you coming with us? And the inevitable answer: Yes.

In those early days of Seabrook Farms, the Seabrook family lived in a house close to the processing and cold storage plants. The area was called, not surprisingly, Farm Center. The housing for Italian workers was across Parsonage Road and down the street from the Seabrook homestead, and Jack Seabrook, who grew up in the house at Farm Central, has fond memories of the immigrant families.

> We Seabrooks were Presbyterians and went to a very plain, unadorned church. As a child, I was fascinated by the contrast with the Roman Catholic Church, with the color and excitement of the religious processions held in the Italian village on saints' days. But there was another reason why I liked the Italian village best. At every event,

saints' days, weddings, funerals, or christenings, there always was a cake soaked in sweet anisette liquor, which we kids loved. I went to these events with my mother, who felt the family should be represented, but I doubt she knew why I was so willing to go. Delivered to our house every morning was wonderful Italian bread baked daily in the brick beehive ovens cooperatively by the ladies in the Italian village. To this day, I don't like store-bought bread."[5]

Over the years, workers from faraway places found their way to Seabrook and the global village by routes that were sometimes dangerous, often circuitous, and, in at least one case, almost inexplicable. The case in question has to do with a group of more than 100 single men who came to Seabrook shortly after World War I and were identified, broadly, as former soldiers in the White Russian Army that had been defeated by the Red Army, the Bolsheviks. How they came to Seabrook is as unclear as the exact nature of American involvement in the Soviet Union, after the Revolution, from the summer of 1918 to April 1919. In July 1918, President Wilson approved a 9,000-man American military expedition to Siberia and north Russia but provided rather fuzzy guidelines as to the role of the troops.[6] Supposedly, they were not to interfere directly in the fighting between the White Army and the Red Army. General William S. Graves, who commanded the American force, wrote years later that he and his men had followed the president's policy, as vague as it was. He also concluded that the lack of solid information about the intentions of the United States and other allied powers "indicate[d] that the various Governments taking part in the intervention [took] very little pride in this venture."[7]

It is possible that the men who made their way to Seabrook came out of the Soviet Union with the American expeditionary force when it withdrew. They may also have been on board one or more of the 100 ships that carried White Army soldiers to Constantinople, where they later dispersed. A final scenario, which may be the most probable, has them migrating through Poland to Germany and hence to America along with thousands of other Russian émigrés.

At Seabrook, the Russians were quartered in old farmhouses that once had been homesteads on the small land parcels Seabrook had been purchasing at a furious rate since 1913. Each of the buildings housing the Russians was called "Polack Hotel" by other workers, who used the pejorative term for persons of Polish ancestry casually, without intending it to be hurtful or deprecating. Most of the Seabrook bosses and timekeepers were unable to pronounce or correctly spell Russian names, so on company records the men showed up as "Joe" or "John" or "Jim." They were excellent workers. One of the more difficult jobs at Seabrook Farms in those days before so much labor intensive work was taken over by machines, involved heaving lima bean and pea vines into a feeder with a long-handled pitchfork. The task required steady, continuous pitching, and the workers had to be careful not to overload or underload the feeder. This job went on from dawn to dusk in the summer heat. The Russians never complained, probably because life at Seabrook was still many times better than it was under either the czars or the Bolsheviks.

Off the job, the Russians kept pretty much to themselves. None of them ever married and, so far as anyone knows, none of them even dated a woman. What they did do was drink alcohol in very large quantities. Prohibition, of course, had become law in 1919, but the men purchased alcohol in five-gallon cans from local bootleggers and mixed it with soda pop. In later years, it was suspected that some of the Russians sneaked into C. F.'s private stock and made off with a much better quality liquor than they had ever before experienced. It is generally believed that C. F. himself was selling applejack illegally. Applejack is made from hard cider, and Seabrook Farms had, at the time, both apple orchards and a not-so-secret distillery.

We get a picture of Seabrook Farms at this time through the eyes of a teenage girl, Sarah Hand. For an assignment at Bridgeton High School, she visited Seabrook in 1921 and wrote an essay, later published in a public relations booklet by the Bridgeton Chamber of Commerce.

> At the present time, [Seabrook Farms] own 4,000 acres of which 300 are under irrigation. Hothouses [numbering]

> six in all, in size 60 x 300 feet (covering ten acres of land), have been erected. There is almost a city there now. To save carting, two railroads have run their tracks through the farm. There is enough business to keep six tractors, 300 horses and mules, seven trucks and a number of Ford cars busy all the time. Mr. Seabrook has built and is still building houses for his men to live in. The cold storage plant will hold 500 carloads. Would you believe it if I told you they have 20,000 bushels of potatoes in cold storage now? It is hard to locate "C. F.," for as soon as he gets home from Philadelphia, he takes the train for New York or some other place; he certainly is one busy man.[8]

At about the same time Sarah was making her observations, the traveling C. F. stayed home long enough to start a company newsletter, which later grew into a newspaper. The first issues of the newsletter had no title, so C. F. announced he would award a gold watch to the person who came up with an acceptable name. Much to his surprise, the winner of the contest was a woman, and he had to come up with another (but undisclosed) prize. The winning title, not very original or clever, was *The Seabrooker.*

As editor and publisher, C. F. took up most of the front page of an early edition to spell out his and, therefore, Seabrook Farms' work ethic.[9]

His statement, boxed by heavy, black lines, began with the heading **"Wanted!"** in boldface. What he wanted, the notice went on to say, were men and women

> who prefer life and work here in the open air, with a home only a few minutes from their work, instead of the shorter hours (and long travel back and forth!) and high wages (and still higher cost of living) in the City. No sulkers or people with touchy feelings need apply. Anyone who says that he can get a job from "so and so" any time

> he wants it had better take it. It is better than this one. Our regular workday is a ten-hour day. However, the work consists in doing whatever the employer feels like asking at any minute of the day or night. Anyone who can meet the above specifications we invite to join our growing organization, which still has room not only at the top, but at the bottom, and halfway up as well.[10]

C. F. signed his name. It may be inconceivable today, but over a span of fifty years, Seabrook Farms never had trouble finding men and women who would work under those terms.

In 1919 an imported blight was wreaking havoc on the majestic American chestnut tree. As a consequence, the United States embargoed the importation of all shrubs and flowers from Europe. The order fell hardest on growers of ornamental plants in Holland. America had become a major outlet for ornamentals and bulbs for such perennials as tulips and narcissus. Peter M. Koster, one of the Dutch nurserymen, had a thriving business in Boskoop that was severely threatened by the embargo. Instead of merely complaining or accepting an uncertain and perhaps disastrous future as some of his colleagues were doing, Koster decided that if he could not export his plants to America, he would export himself.[11]

However, he did not come alone. He obtained a special permit from the U.S. Horticultural Board that allowed him to bring over a number of crates of roses, azaleas, and rhododendrons that were certified free of insects and disease. It is unclear how he knew in advance about Cumberland County, but that is where he finally settled, on some thirty acres in Woodruff, a crossroads located two or three miles southeast of Seabrook. C. F. quickly took note of Koster's little nursery and persuaded the nurseryman to enter into partnership with him and move his business to Seabrook land on Highway 77 at its intersection with Polk Lane. The relationship between Koster and C. F. remained close, but the business never became part of corporate Seabrook Farms. C. F. also totally owned the Seabrook Bulb Gardens, which he began, perhaps not coincidentally, at about the same time Koster arrived in the area with his crates.

Inevitably, Koster's Nursery and Seabrook Bulb Gardens together attracted more Dutch nurserymen, and they and their families added a western European flavor to the growing global village. Of those who immigrated, many later went on to start their own nurseries. Among those who made the voyage to America were Jan and Jack Vermullen, Klaas and Jack Akerboom, Herbert Hoogendoorn, and Cornelius, Neil, Gerard, and Ted Overdevest. In the 2001 Yellow Pages for Cumberland County, under the heading "Nurseries—Plants,Trees, etc.," the name leading the list is Akerboom Nurseries, Inc.

Both the Seabrook Bulb Gardens and Koster's Nursery flourished far beyond the imagination of either Koster or C. F. At the Seabrook Gardens, located near the Koster Nursery and, eventually, next door to the Seabrook estate on Polk Lane, 250 acres of golden daffodils, sixty varieties of tulips, and thirty-five varieties of narcissus not only produced fresh flowers to be shipped far and wide, but also constituted an incredibly spectacular display that attracted numerous sightseers each spring. Koster became one of the nation's most prodigious growers of ornamental shrubs. Arguably, his nursery's greatest achievement was the Koster Blue Spruce. Never grown or even known in the region before Koster's time, it is now a prized, and expensive, evergreen found throughout the East.

In the June, 1923 edition of *Farm and Farmside,* C. F. outlined his rules for what was called "intensive" or "corporate" farming: First, accommodate the business to its locale, particularly in regard to growing season and distance from market. Second, take on only what the owner and workers can handle. Third, the head of the business must take personal charge of all aspects "because the first nine-tenths of the job is entirely spending money and labor, and if there is any breakdown, even at the harvesting and marketing end, the result is a loss." Fourth, "keep every acre busy all the time, follow early crops with late ones on the same ground, and sometimes a third crop"; get rid of weeds and unnecessary hedges and fences. "Old-fashioned farming has thousands of acres idle the whole or part of a season taken up with fences and hedges, uncared for old fruit trees, [and] small fenced-in plots seldom used."[12]

There is general agreement that C. F. adhered to his own philosophy, with the possible exception of his admonition about taking on only what can efficiently be handled. As noted in Chapter 1, in the 1920s, C. F., flush with new capital and obsessed with his self-taught engineering skills, went overboard erecting buildings of all sorts. Speaking of how C. F. took "personal charge of all aspects" of the business, son Jack said that his father "had the most incredible amount of energy that anybody ever had. And he was dogged and single-minded. What he wanted, he wanted, and he would move Heaven and Earth to get it. Fortunately for all of us, a lot of time what he wanted was the right thing."

The early 1920s were a heady time at Seabrook Farms. Expansion was rampant: more acreage, more workers, more buildings, more varieties of vegetables and fruits. Jack Seabrook remembers what it was like when he was just a youngster growing up amid all the "more":

> There were great sights, sounds and smells everywhere at Farm Center for us kids. Just across the street from our house was a stable with 200 horses and, right in front of the house, a Frick refrigeration plant powered by a row of magnificent Corliss steam engines with showy snap valves and gleaming, shiny pistons, all in rhythmic motion. On still nights, the ammonia fumes from the compressors mingled with the ammonia from the stables. The effect was like a whiff of smelling salts. The Blacksmith shop was nearby with four forges glowing, where John Shaw sweated next to Abe Skilowitz, both pounding red hot iron, with the smell of soft coal smoke and burning hooves. The sawmill made whole logs into shipping boxes and smelled of pine. The machine shop, smelling of hot machine oil, was dominated by Germans. Schmidt, the boss, told exciting stories of chasing Pancho Villa in Mexico as a soldier with General "Black Jack" Pershing. When I was a little older and rode the midnight trucks to the New York flower

> market, I even learned a little Yiddish. We never thought about segregation or integration. My two best friends were Paul, the son of black migrants from South Carolina, and Presto, the son of Sicilian immigrants. It was all part of a wonderful education for C.F.'s three sons.[13]

But suddenly, or so it seemed, more became less, and the less unfortunately resulted from lack of money. It was a classic, textbook case of what happens when management, in this instance C. F., doesn't pay close enough attention to the two ledger columns, and the expenses column forces the income column into red ink. By the autumn of 1924, the White family in New York and others who had bankrolled C. F. since 1913, and who now owned a controlling interest in the business, were paying very close attention to the Seabrook Farms ledger, and they did not like what they saw. They were so dismayed, in fact, that they told C. F. he was no longer their man, no longer in charge of the operation they effectively owned, and they put the business in receivership and under new management.

The new management team, headed by Warren W. Oley, who held the title General Superintendent, answered to a new board of directors and the receiver, Meyer Handelman of New York. Perhaps the greatest blow to C. F.'s pride was the renaming of the business he had almost single-handedly nurtured for the past eleven years. Seabrook Farms overnight, or so it seemed, became Del-Bay Farms.

Del-Bay Farms lost no time capitalizing on what Seabrook Farms had already accomplished. In 1924 the new team published a promotional brochure that invited one and all to visit "the largest diversified farm in the East." The brochure suggested that the best time to stop by would be mid to late April, when 46,000 peach trees would be in blossom and acres of tulips and narcissus would carpet the countryside. A little later in the spring, 70,000 apple trees would blanket 650 acres in fragrant white petals. The publication also brought readers up-to-date on the company's infrastructure, the high cost of which over a relatively short period of time had helped to put Seabrook Farms into receivership. In that year, 1924, at the start of what turned out to be a fairly short life span for Del-Bay Farms, the company described its assets without once mentioning they had all been inherited—lock, stock, and goodwill: Employees number 700 at the height of the growing season. The workforce, most of whom live in "company homes located in groups or scattered over the farm area," includes Italians, Germans, Poles, Hollanders, Swedes, and Russians. Employees' children attend "one of the most modern rural school buildings in South Jersey," and everyone enjoys "a modern building with facilities for recreation and education."

In the three years since the teenage Sarah Hand visited Seabrook Farms, the number of horses and mules had decreased from 300 to 100, trucks and cars had increased to forty, and three tractors had been added, bringing the total to ten. If Sarah had returned in 1924, she would have discovered that at least one of her observations of 1921 was still valid. C. F. was "still hard to locate." He was traveling the world as a successful if novice civil engineer, so whatever Del-Bay did to or for his Seabrook Farms, C. F. was hardly ever present either to cheer or jeer from the sidelines.

As late as the mid-1980s, New Jersey boasted that its farm income per acre was among the highest of all the states', even though only one percent of the state's population was engaged in farming and New Jersey was then, as it is now, the most urbanized state in the nation.[14] The apparent anomaly surprises many people today, when so much of our fresh fruit and vegetables originate in California, Florida, and countries south of our border, where the growing season is nearly year-round. However, even today New Jersey ranks fourth in peach production, just behind Georgia, despite the fact that the Seabrook Farms orchards planted by C. F. in the early part of the last century are no longer standing to add to the 8,000 productive acres of trees in the state, according to the Rutgers University Research Center.

At Seabrook Farms, the time for planting and the time for plucking what was planted extended from late March to late October. Spinach was the first crop picked in spring and the last one harvested in October, because spinach picked in the spring was planted in the fall and the seeds of fall spinach went into the ground in April.

When Del-Bay Farms reported in 1924 that "the minimum number of Del-Bay employees during the year is 200 and the maximum 700," it was referring to the reality of farming in South Jersey then and in the years after C. F. regained control. Many hands—nonsulkers all—were required during the months of sowing, reaping, and processing, but significantly fewer were needed during the months when the fields lay cold and hard and the last produce had been shipped from cold storage. Aside from necessary maintenance and making any needed repairs to equipment, one of the few chores for permanent workers—those who remained in company housing all year—during the winter was cutting wood for the stoves that heated their quarters.

By the late 1930s permanent employees who were laid off for most or all of the winter months were paid from unemployment insurance, but government assistance was not available in the 1920s. However, then and even later when unemployment insurance was enacted into law, permanent employees often accepted part-time work in nearby stores or plants that operated all year.

During the 1920s, urban dwellers, many of them recent immigrants, constituted most of the temporary workforce. A number of these seasonal workers commuted daily between their homes in Philadelphia and Camden and the fields of South Jersey. Italian American day pickers residing in Philadelphia, for example, were recruited and supervised by a fellow Italian American called a padrone. Seabrook Farms (and Del-Bay Farms during its tenure) dealt with the padrone, paying him so much to deliver so many workers. The padrone, in turn, paid the workers in his cadre according to the number of bushels picked or on the basis of some other standard for measuring work performed. Seasonal workers who were not from nearby cities generally stayed in rude barracks.

Migrant workers from southern states, most of whom stayed only through the growing season, did not arrive at Del-Bay/Seabrook Farms in any significant numbers until the beginning of the Depression. By 1929, however, Cumberland County employed more migrant workers for more days than all New Jersey counties except Burlington. An increasing number of these seasonal workers were African Americans from southern states, and at the same time, African American day pickers from nearby cities and towns were beginning to take the place of recent immigrants from Italy who had commuted from South Philadelphia. The African Americans adopted the Italian American work model; that is, a group would work under a unit leader much like the padrone of the old system.[15]

The Depression uprooted thousands of American families throughout the land, and many of them became transplants in places quite distant from where they had once lived and worked. Thousands more, primarily in the South, although they did not move elsewhere permanently, became part of a growing wave of migrant labor that rolled north in early spring to work at places like Seabrook Farms and then receded toward home in the fall. Willard A. Heaps described this movement for young people more than twenty years after the south-north migration peaked:

> Every year in the late spring and early summer months, literally thousands of buses, often dilapidated inside and out, move northward on our nation's major arterial highways. Additional thousands of automobiles, almost always used cars and often models of a decade or more past, join the flow, always in a northerly direction. Though not readily identifiable in the interstate traffic on the highways and turnpikes, they are a familiar—and welcome—sight on the less-traveled roads in the rural areas where the largest farms are located. Often their destination is reached by secondary unpaved and dusty roads.[16]

Jack Seabrook is convinced that the used car is more responsible for how America and Americans grew up in the twentieth century than we know. "When you think about it, in Europe most people who owned a car kept it forever, and there was hardly any secondhand car market," he said. "Consequently, only people with a fair amount of money could own their own automobile, which is one of the reasons their labor force was never mobile. It just wasn't practical. America, on the other hand, developed the used car market, and that totally changed the character of all kinds of things, the migrant labor stream being just one of them. I had a Model A Ford in college, and I remember distinctly that gasoline cost me eleven cents a gallon. You could go a hell of a long way on a dollar's worth of gasoline."

At the end of 1929, just about the time the Depression began, C. F. returned to Seabrook. He had been traveling far and wide for his engineering/construction company, building roads and all manner of other facilities for countries in Central America and Europe, principally Russia. He came home in time to learn that Del-Bay Farms, after five years, was giving up and that he could buy back the business and reclaim the name Seabrook Farms. He still owned 1,000 acres, so what he needed to purchase from Del-Bay was its 3,400 acres and, of course, the processing and cold storage plants, and the attendant equipment and machinery. No one, except C. F. of course, wanted to purchase land in those hard times getting harder, so the acreage from Del-Bay came dirt cheap—almost literally. "Cash was king. For a few thousand dollars cash, C. F. was able first to lease, then to purchase from [the] receiver . . . the entire plant and equipment of the cannery established by New York Canners at Farm Center some years before."[17]

The times called for shrewdness bordering on miracle working, and C. F. and his sons were up to the challenge. First, they conceived a plan whereby they gathered up mounds of cabbage they could not sell on the market, built a small plant that converted the cabbage into sauerkraut, then sold the sauerkraut to the State of New Jersey for distribution to poor families. Not content with pulling off one neat trick for survival, C. F. and his oldest son, Belford, got an idea that they could purchase dust bowl cattle from the Midwest which would otherwise perish, and potatoes and carrots that were destined to rot on the ground, and turn all those ingredients into beef stew.

Belford pulled one last rabbit out of the hat. Seabrook Farms contracted with the State Highway Department to remove snow from state roads during the winter. "The State did not have the equipment or the personnel to clear its new network of highways, and [Seabrook Farms] had little work for its trucks, tractors, and skilled operators and mechanics."[18] Fortunately for the Seabrook men, it snowed a lot in those early winters of the Depression. They received seventy-five cents an hour from the state at a time when the best Seabrook could pay was twenty or thirty cents an hour. It was a blessed marriage.

Unfortunately, however, the state treasury was itself running low, and eventually the state could no longer pay for the food products Seabrook Farms was turning out for the emergency relief effort. The American Can Company, which supplied tin cans for the cannery, agreed to wait a year for payment, and the dwindling number of Seabrook employees were sometimes paid in script. Everyone was finally bailed out when John T. Dorrance Sr., founder of the Campbell Soup Company located in Camden, died and his estate made a huge inheritance tax payment to the state. Seabrook was once again "a happy place."[19]

But not for long.

C. F. Seabrook and his sons, the summer of 1951.
Left to right: Jack, Belford, C. F., and Courtney

Aerial view of the global village (circa 1951). The original Italian Village is to the immediate right of the water tower, with housing for the Tennessee and Jamaican workers directly behind it. The four rows of houses stretching east from the smokestack are West Village and Gunnison Village.

In the background at far right are Hoover Village and Hoover Village Annex. The federal project apartments and dormitories are in the center background, and the few homes to the right of and behind the school (upper left) make up School Village.

The Italian Village (circa 1909), in place before the main factory was built.

Donald Norimatsu at Hoover Village Annex (circa 1945), the rude housing that Japanese Americans initially found as dismal as the internment camps in which they had been forced to live during World War II.

Fresh produce being loaded from the “wash house” (circa 1917).
This white brick building became the Murphy bulk freezer after 1933.

Picking wax beans (circa 1944).

Bean pickers during the World War II years, getting baskets weighed and checked.

At Seabrook Farms, children as young as twelve picked beans.

Iceberg lettuce being harvested and crated during World War II. (Notice the overhead irrigation system.)

String beans being harvested by machine during World War II.

Hoppers and hoppers of peas ready to be washed, sorted, blanched, and packed (circa 1952).

Sorting corn on the cob for processing (circa 1952).

Shift change at the Seabrook Farms processing plant, 1952.

Workers coming off the night shift, at right, heading down Parsonage Road toward home. Day shift workers, at left, walk toward the plant to put in their ten or twelve hours, 1952.

Chapter 3

Finding a Better Way

Happiness was in short supply across the United States in the early 1930s, and the results of the Depression were felt no more keenly than on America's farms. In 1932 a newspaper reporter likened American farm workers to Mongolian peasants. Prices for agricultural products had not been so low, some said, since the reign of Queen Elizabeth I. A bushel of corn sold for seven cents, and a box of 200 apples brought forty cents. A grain farmer who went to market with a wagonload of oats came home without enough money to buy his child a pair of four-dollar shoes.[1]

The hard times produced bitter fruit, in abundance, and in 1934 Seabrook Farms was forced to share in that harvest. Despite their best intentions and schemes, the Seabrooks were hard-pressed to find jobs for all those who wanted and needed them and to pay wages that workers rightly deserved. In that middle year of the Depression, in addition to the collapse of the economy, at least two other elements added to the general malaise felt both in industry and in agriculture, especially in an industrialized agricultural operation like Seabrook Farms. One element was bad blood and feuding between the AFL and CIO, who, at the time, were separate and rival labor organizations. The second element was the Communist Party's exploitation of the existing disillusionment and unrest within the nation's labor force.

C. F. was a fairly typical employer at the time: paternalistic and anti-union, but, according to prevailing business standards, fair. Most farm workers, including those employed at Seabrook, were not represented by any union. However, Seabrook had been forced into an under-the-table deal with a local Teamsters union, which, the Seabrooks alleged, was tied to the New York mafia. The Teamsters belonged to the AFL. Under the arrangement, Seabrook Farms purchased from the local a certain number of paid-up-dues books with spaces for union members' names left blank. When a Seabrook truck loaded with produce arrived at the Holland Tunnel on its way to the New York market, the driver would surrender one of the books to a union agent at the mouth of the tunnel. The union implied, not too subtly, that if a Seabrook driver didn't have one of the books, something unpleasant might happen to the truck, the truck's contents, or, possibly, the driver.[2]

The Agricultural and Cannery Workers Industrial Union operated under the CIO banner. Donald and Eleanor Henderson of New York City and Leif and Vivian Dahl of nearby Vineland were organizers for the union in the spring of 1934. Donald Henderson had been fired from his position in the economics department at Columbia University because he was a member of the Communist Party. On the strength of that fact, as well as information about Communist infiltration of the labor movement revealed years later, the Seabrook family remains convinced that what occurred at Seabrook Farms in the spring and summer of 1934 was contrived and paid for by the Communist Party on orders direct from Moscow.

The trouble started with an unwitting or intentional misunderstanding concerning the wages to be paid to Seabrook employees. The workers, through their spokespersons, claimed that Seabrook Farms had first agreed to pay male seasonal workers thirty cents an hour and female workers (most of whom worked in the cannery) twenty-five cents an hour, but were now planning to renege on that agreement and actually reduce wages to seventeen cents an hour for both men and women.[3]

According to other accounts of labor conditions at New Jersey farms at that time, Seabrook was probably paying wages above those being offered elsewhere, not that the company had any reason to boast. Ever since the late 1920s and early 1930s, many of the seasonal workers at Seabrook Farms were African Americans and Italian Americans, a number of the latter group being recent immigrants. As noted in the previous chapter, state relief provisions for unemployed laborers were unreliable; the state sometimes pleaded poverty along with the people out of work.

This less-than-satisfactory relief program most often hurt African Americans. Ewing Township outside Trenton, for example, actually issued begging licenses to African Americans suddenly dropped from relief rolls. In southern farming counties, including Cumberland, "farmers who sought cheap labor gleefully offered fifteen and twenty cents an hour as wages to family heads who could no longer claim assistance from the public treasury."[4]

C. F. maintained that there was no plan to reduce wages, but he admitted he could not make good on a promise to raise wages because the terms of a loan he had negotiated with the Reconstruction Finance Corporation forbade the company from using the funds to increase workers' pay. The loan, he said, was intended to help Seabrook Farms get through the season. The success of the 1934 season was in grave doubt when, in June, the Hendersons and Dahls called Seabrook workers out on strike. The Seabrook family contended that many of the strikers were not even employed by Seabrook Farms. "Large numbers of homeless people were moved from the cities of Newark and Philadelphia into the empty barracks-style housing that had been built during the boom years to house seasonal temporary workers. Most of these squatters had never been employed at Seabrook Farms, and there was no work for them now, but they provided mass pickets to support attempted strikes."[5]

Although planting, harvesting, and canning that spring continued on a reduced scale, the atmosphere at Seabrook Farms was tense, always on the verge of becoming ugly. Jack Seabrook, who was seventeen years old in 1934, remembers carrying a pistol in his left armpit, and the company organized its own complement of guards, which was, in turn, backed up by local police forces and the county Sheriff's Department.[6]

Occasional strikes persisted throughout most of June and into July. Jack Seabrook recalls being trained by plain-clothes state troopers in how to use a club. The clubs he and his brothers had were spokes from old wagon wheels. "I can remember a sergeant saying, 'Now, never raise your club, because some damn photographer from the *New York Times* will take a picture of you. Keep it low and jam the guy in the crotch. Then, when the *New York Times* takes a picture, you'll see everybody bowing to you.' And it worked."

Robert Busnardo's grandfather was an Italian immigrant who came to Seabrook Farms from the Pennsylvania coal mines in the late 1920s, and his son (Robert's father) was in his late teens when the strikes started. He came home from the picket line one day to find his house in the so-called Italian Village at Farm Center vacant. Neighbors said that Seabrook Farms people had come by and cleaned out the house and loaded all the furniture onto a flatbed truck. "What they did was ride around Bridgeton until they found an empty house," said Busnardo, "and then they dumped all the stuff in front of that house. If the owner didn't want to rent the house, tough." The Seabrooks prevailed on the owner. That's where the Busnardo family lived for the duration of the strikes.

The unrest turned violent on the morning of July 9, when Seabrook Farms tractors and trucks moved up the highway to enter the fields and begin the harvesting of beets. Hundreds of strikers who were gathered at the main entrance to the fields began hurling rocks and sticks at the tractor and truck drivers. Sheriff's deputies, aided by local farmers who were under contract to Seabrook and had been deputized as a sort of vigilante group, attacked the strikers. They, along with local police and firemen, used tear gas, nauseating gas, and fire hoses. "The gas and streams of water from fire hoses were the principal weapons of the Sheriff's men, but they inflicted almost as much discomfort on their users as on the strikers. Frequently, the opposing sides were so mixed up that gas and water fell on friend and foe alike." A local policeman was the only person treated for exposure to the gas. No one on either side was seriously hurt, but twenty-six strikers were arrested, including Eleanor Henderson, one of the organizers.[7]

Robert Busnardo recalls his father telling him that he was one of the strikers arrested July 9 for allegedly cutting one of the strikebreakers with a knife. "My dad was in jail with another man. He said they got up in front of the judge, and the judge said, 'You guys are accused of cutting this man.' My dad said, 'I didn't cut him.' The other guy said, 'Sir, I cut him.' The judge replied, 'You know you could have killed this man.' The guy said, 'No sir, I didn't give him but that much of the knife [indicating not much more than the tip]. I knowed I was gonna cut him, but I didn't wanna kill him.'"

Depending on what report of the day's events one reads or hears, either a tear gas canister set a workers' barracks on fire or strikers deliberately set it ablaze. In any case, the building burned to the ground. In the afternoon a truckload of beets headed for the cannery was attacked by a small group of men and women wielding rocks. That incident ended the day's rioting, and the sun set on a grim scene: barbed wire barricades; fields and roads littered with spent gas canisters, rocks, and bricks and armed guards patrolling the cannery and other buildings, including the Seabrook family home.[8]

That night, while strikers attended a mass meeting to hear organizers call for a continuance of the strike against "capitalism," C. F. fired off a telegram to Governor A. Harry Moore:

> REGARDING THE STATEMENT MADE BY CERTAIN NEWSPAPERS THAT THE STRIKE AT SEABROOK FARMS WAS DUE TO A REDUCTION IN WAGES, I WISH TO ADVISE THAT NO REDUCTION IN WAGES HAD BEEN MADE AND NONE IS CONTEMPLATED AT THE

PRESENT TIME. A SHORT TIME PRIOR TO THE STRIKE, IT WAS NECESSARY TO REDUCE OUR FORCE AND LAY OFF A LARGE NUMBER OF TEMPORARY LABORERS BROUGHT IN TO DO SEASONAL WORK. THE REASON FOR THIS WAS PARTLY ON ACCOUNT OF THE WORK BEING FINISHED AND PARTLY BECAUSE THE PREVAILING LOW PRICES MADE IT UNPROFITABLE TO HARVEST CERTAIN CROPS. IT WAS ALSO NECESSARY, DUE TO ECONOMIC CONDITIONS, TO MAKE A REDUCTION IN THE ACREAGE OF CERTAIN FALL CROPS.

C. F. repeated the Seabrooks' charge that the strikes were called "by the Communist labor agitators." The strike, he said, was not called by Seabrooks' employees. He stated that management was more than willing to meet with any committee of "[the company's] regular employees."[9]

The next day, July 10, John A. Moffit, a federal mediator sent from Washington, worked out an agreement whereby men and women for whom the company had jobs could return without prejudice and at the same wages they had received before the strike. Both sides also agreed to the appointment of an impartial board to settle any future disputes. At a mass meeting of strikers, Donald Henderson, the chief organizer for the Agricultural Canners Industrial Union, and the one person the Seabrooks were certain was a Communist agent, mounted a soapbox and urged employees to reject the settlement. However, David L. Horuvitz, counsel to the union, jumped up on the same soapbox and shouted, "Now, boys, tell me, man to man, do you really want to go back to work?" The crowded shouted, "Yes," and most of the workers headed for the company offices to sign the roster as returning employees. When Henderson tried to stop them, a phalanx of former strikers turned on him, yelling, "Throw him out of here; he's caused enough trouble!" Henderson finally was whisked away by local police; he never returned.[10]

Later that summer of 1934, the *Journal of Negro Life* lauded the strike at Seabrook Farms as testament to the fact that black and white workers could join together. "There is a feeling of satisfaction among Negroes, strikers and non-strikers, that the demonstration was made, no matter what the immediate results might be."[11] A number of African American workers had been displaced during the early stages of the strike, before the climax on July 9, and some of them appeared at so-called transient offices run by the state's Emergency Relief Administration (ERA). Perhaps typical of the case histories of seasonal African American workers during the Depression, as recorded by the ERA during June 1934, is the story of a man identified as Mr. J. He was born in Jonesville, Louisiana, in 1912, so he was twenty-two at the time of the strike. His parents, who were farmers, had moved the family to Monroe, Louisiana, where he went to school through the fifth grade. He left school to work at odd jobs. When he was in his teens, he drifted north, eventually finding his way to Bridgeton. The ERA reported as follows: "Mr. J. worked for two months at Seabrook Farms. He had been out of work before applying for relief because of a strike. After the strike is entirely settled, he expects to earn enough to purchase a ticket back home [to Louisiana]."[12]

After the strike, Belford and Jack Seabrook saw the handwriting on the wall, even if C. F. didn't, and the writing spelled out in big black letters "UNIONS ARE HERE TO STAY." They finally convinced the Old Man that one honest union they could negotiate with fairly would be more likely to keep peace among workers than a series of locals, not of the Seabrooks' choosing, that could come along periodically and stir up trouble among employees, such as the CIO's Agricultural Canners Industrial Union. In the late 1930s, James Flanigan headed the Pennsylvania Labor Relations Board, which was the first such body in the nation. The Seabrooks got to meet him through John B. Kelly, father of actress Grace Kelly, who was influential among bricklayers in Philadelphia. Following Flanigan's advice, the Seabrooks negotiated with the AFL Butchers and Teamsters Unions throughout the rest of the decade. By 1941, Seabrook Farms became an AFL closed shop. The Teamsters were free to organize truck drivers and employees who worked in the garages and warehouse. The Butchers had jurisdiction over everyone else except office workers, including all seasonal workers. When the AFL announced the deal in its newspaper, it stated, "Repeated CIO efforts to organize Seabrook Farms met with rebuff. The ultra-radical slogan of 'down with the bosses' didn't work with Seabrook employees."[13] An article in the January

1944 edition of *Reader's Digest* labeled Seabrook Farms "the first big farm to unionize in this country."[14]

While the Seabrooks were finding a better way to treat their employees and head off labor problems, they were also finding a better way to package and sell the vegetables and fruits they were raising on an increasing number of acres (by 1940, nearly 20,000 acres either owned outright by Seabrook Farms or by small farms under contract to the company). The new way of production was quick freezing, a process that had been invented earlier by Clarence Birdseye and with which Belford and Jack Seabrook had been experimenting. When, in the late 1930s, C. F. concluded a contract with General Foods to produce frozen vegetables and fruits under the Birdseye label, Seabrook Farms, which was to become the leader in so many aspects of the agri-industry, was then the only company in America turning out high-quality frozen vegetables in large quantities. "The old varieties of vegetables used for the fresh market or canning were not suitable for freezing, but Seabrook Farms knew how to quickly develop and use new varieties in commercial quantity. Seabrook Farms also had the land, the know-how, the management skills, a processing plant, and complete control of the entire process from seed to package. This greatly shortened the development period for Birdseye, and soon high-quality quick-frozen vegetables were in the stores. This early start made Birdseye the dominant brand for years."[15]

The frozen food business changed Seabrook Farms forever, and the men and women who remained with the company after the labor strife of 1934 were destined to earn considerably more during their productive years than nearly any other agricultural workers in the United States. One of those who prospered was William J.Scheffer, who, at age sixteen, rode with the Hungarian Home Guard to defeat a Communist uprising in Budapest during World War I. He arrived at Seabrook at the height of the July 1934 rioting. He had read about the trouble in the *New York Times,* taking particular note of references to alleged Communist influence. He decided to drive down from New York City where he was working and living at the time and see for himself what was going on. Jack Seabrook remembered their first meeting: "I, [then] a high school senior, was circulating anonymously among the mob trying to spot the leaders when I saw this dark, muscular, handsome foreigner with a black mustache and promptly assumed he must be one of the main 'agitators.'" After Scheffer explained why he was there, Jack took him to see C. F., "who was instantly impressed with this well-educated, erect, smart, heel-clicking former Hussar." Scheffer held almost all of the top management positions at Seabrook Farms over the next twenty-five years. He was all spit and polish, and he barked orders to workers like a drill sergeant, but "he was a genius, full of ideas on how to measure any kind of output and use that measurement as a tool for managing." Scheffer got along equally well with C. F. and all three sons, no small feat, and his only failing, if it could be called that, was that he never quite understood the modern American system whereby management and labor negotiated pay and working conditions. "We were careful to keep him away from the union leaders," Jack wrote.[16]

As the world drifted hopelessly toward war in Europe and Asia, Seabrook Farms was moving purposefully and swiftly toward becoming the leader in the frozen food business. The building boom of the 1920s that C. F. had engineered and which had led in part to his eventually losing the business for a half decade, now resumed in earnest as the company expanded to accommodate more vegetable assembly lines, refrigeration compressors, and cold storage facilities. Indeed, the demand for compressors probably saved the Frick factory in Waynesboro, Pennsylvania, which had been on the verge of shutting down its compressor manufacturing operations. The building frenzy required Seabrook Farms to hire hundreds of year-round construction workers and many more men and women to work in the fields and plants. "In the 1930s, once freezing commenced, Seabrook was the brightest spot in the economy of southern New Jersey. Employment rose rapidly and wages followed."[17]

Because of the rapid expansion, Seabrook Farms needed more land, but whatever cash the company had was going to pay for the burgeoning building program, additional workers' salaries, and the materials and equipment necessary to plant and harvest crops. Even though land was still very cheap in the latter half of the 1930s, Seabrook Farms could not afford to buy all the acreage it needed to keep up with the new demands of the freezing business. One approach to solving the problem was to buy acres and then promptly lease them to investors, thereby covering most of the original purchase price. One of the major investors was Betty Fleishman Holmes, heir to the creator of Fleishman yeast and other products, who leased land through three trusts set up for her three children. Most of the land obtained through Holmes's trusts consisted of small farms in adjacent Salem County whose mortgages had been foreclosed by local banks

By 1939, in addition to marketing frozen vegetables under the Birdseye label, Seabrook Farms was also packaging under its own label and for two dozen or so other customers. At about the same time, Seabrook Farms formed a Canadian company, Deerfield Packing Limited, to produce frozen vegetables and fruits primarily for markets in Great Britain. The new company employed French Canadians and Native Americans, thereby adding to the multicultural mix of Seabrook Farms, even though they were far removed from the growing global village in Cumberland County.

Among those men and women joining the ever-larger workforce and taking up residence in the global village were transplants from the foothills of the Great Smoky Mountains in Tennessee. Although the splendid forests that clothed that southern range of the Appalachians appeared lush and soft, life in the valleys was hard and getting harder in the late 1930s and early 1940s. What industry there was in places like Newport and Greeneville, and it was never much, had been hit hard by the Depression, and families in little towns like Carson Spring, Parrottsville and Bybee were jobless—and looking north.

No one knows for certain who first came to Seabrook Farms from that part of the country, although Ernest "Dooley" Holt thinks it might have been a family by the name of Shelton. By the early 1940s, perhaps 200 men, women, and children had trekked to South Jersey by jalopy and open truck. Still others would come from Appalachia after World War II; some would be actively recruited by Seabrook Farms and would arrive in Seabrook buses. No matter when they came or what town they came from, no matter what their previous employment may have been or what grade they had completed in school, they all were known ever after to other residents of the global village as "hillbillies."

Whoever arrived and stayed and liked his or her work—and especially the paycheck—usually contacted relatives and friends back home and said, in effect, "C'mon up!" Among the early arrivals were the Bruce Clarks, including two-year-old Clara, who vaguely remembers the journey from her own experience, young as she was, and whose memory has no doubt been enhanced by what her parents and older siblings told her about the move. Her father came to Seabrook ahead of the family, in about 1939, to see whether he liked the working conditions and to check out living arrangements. After three months he was evidently pleased enough on all counts to return to Tennessee and pack up his family and bring them back with him to Seabrook.

"We had a big truck, and most of us kids were in the back with the furniture. I'll never forget when we got to Seabrook," Clara Clark said. The Clark family was placed in one of the small houses that constituted what people knew then as the Italian Village, off Parsonage Road in Farm Center. "When my father went to back down the main street in the village, it looked to me like the longest road I'd ever seen. In fact, it was, and that vision has never left my mind."

Rufus Hill grew up in a town close to the North Carolina border, on the side of Round Mountain. As he described it, it wasn't exactly a town; it was a place, a crossroads. In the mid-1940s, word was getting back to the hills that jobs could be had in South Jersey; Seabrook Farms needed workers. Rufus, who was single at the time, chipped in with a friend to buy a used Model A Ford, and they headed north. The two men got work immediately, Rufus as a mechanic in one of the garages and his friend as an apprentice electrician. When winter came and the crops were all in and processed, these men, like almost all temporary workers and many permanent employees, were laid off. Instead of doing what many others did during the winter months, take a part-time job or collect unemployment insurance, Rufus and his friend returned to Tennessee. That was December 1947. The following spring, he returned to Seabrook, this time with his new wife.

Rufus's son Ken remembers growing up in two rooms at 46 Hoover Village, a rude barracks that were part of the global village—the company town. The next-door neighbors on one side were Cuban, and an African American family lived on the other side. "The ethnic backgrounds of everybody—that's what I really enjoyed," Hill said. His father moved up the ladder, becoming a stockroom supervisor and transportation dispatcher for the Viner and Transportation Department. Viners were machines that separated peas and beans from their vines. One of Rufus's tasks as dispatcher was to drive to the Philadelphia airport to pick up labels flown in by a customer for whom Seabrook was processing frozen vegetables.

Ernest "Dooley" Holt, Clara Clark's husband, had begun making moonshine in the Smokies in the late 1940s, when he was fourteen. Three years later, in August, he quit high school and, with a borrowed twenty-dollar bill, headed north to Seabrook Farms, the place people in his neck of the Cherokee National Forest talked about a lot. He figured any job there would pay more than he could earn distilling moonshine in the mountains.

He arrived with twelve dollars left from the twenty and took a room in the cinder block dormitories off Route 77 and adjacent to the much less desirable Hoover Village, where the Hills lived. Unfortunately, he said, no one clued him in about the company cafeteria, so he spent most of the twelve dollars on food during the first two weeks. "But I earned eighty-four and a half cents an hour that summer, working twelve-hour days, six days a week. I cleared sixty dollars and eighty-four cents the first week." It was more money than he could have dreamed of back in Appalachia watching corn "likker" dripping through copper tubing.

At the end of World War II, John Melchiorre, who had worked for the Dutch nurseryman Gerard Overdevest at Seabrook Farms as a youngster, came home from the army and was soon hired as a recruiter of seasonal help. One of his first tours of duty was in Logan County, West Virginia. The coal mines of Appalachia were faring as badly as the industries down the mountain chain in Tennessee. Melchiorre came into the hills and hollows of the Mountain State with an offer to men accustomed to breathing black dust: an opportunity to suck in the hot, humid air that draped South Jersey almost every summer. He had no trouble signing them up.

His modus operandi began with a call to the West Virginia Department of Labor. "Someone there would tell me where to go to recruit men. He would say, 'We have a place here in West Virginia where unemployment is very, very bad, and we would like you to go down there if you think it's okay.' Then he would give me the telephone number of a local employment office, say in Logan County, and tell me to call the manager there the next day [perhaps Tuesday or Wednesday]. Meantime, the person at the state office would call ahead to the local office and tell them I would be in touch tomorrow and that I wanted them to place some help wanted ads in local newspapers on Thursday." Melchiorre and another person from Seabrook would interview job applicants all day on Friday and wind up hiring fifty to seventy men before dusk. The next day, Saturday, a Seabrook bus would pull up in front of the employment office, and the new employees would board for the long haul back to South Jersey. If the men stayed the entire season, Seabrook paid their way back to West Virginia.

It seems that Seabrook Farms could never get enough seasonal help in the 1940s, either men to work in the fields and cold storage or women to work in the processing plant. From 1943 to 1946, recruiting efforts extended into the Deep South and zeroed in on female African American college students. Toward the end of May, in each of these years, Seabrook hired thirty or more women and flew them north out of Atlanta, accompanied by chaperones supplied by the company. Eula Johnson, then a sophomore at Clark College in Atlanta, was among the last group hired in 1946. Johnson described the trip: "We flew to Philadelphia in an army plane Seabrook had chartered. It had jump seats along the sides; we thought of ourselves as paratroopers getting ready to jump." The plane was met in Philadelphia by a Seabrook bus.

At Seabrook, the women were housed rent-free in Hoover Village barracks, six persons to a large room with bunk beds. Like other residents of the Village, they used a central toilet and shower. The women worked in the processing plant sorting vegetables and fruits on conveyor belts: peas, string beans, spinach, strawberries, corn, and beets. All except the beets were on their way to being frozen; the beets were canned. The young women put in ten- or twelve-hour days, alternating between day and night shifts. In 1946, the African American college students worked side by side with Caucasian women from Appalachia and Japanese American women who had joined the workforce beginning in 1944. The first week of September, the students packed their bags and headed back to Atlanta and college by train. Again, their transportation was paid, so each woman began the new college term with enough money to help her afford tuition, room, and board.

It should come as no surprise that thirty or so single African American women would attract the attention of single African American men in the area, including workers who had come from the West Indies. Samah Pearson, from Jamaica, was responsible for meeting many of the needs of other Jamaicans working in the fields. One day he entered the plant where Eula was working and introduced himself. In the days that followed, Samah and Eula attended events at the Community House, where Samah, an accomplished guitarist, frequently took part in talent shows. By the end of that summer Samah had proposed marriage. Eula's father, who himself lived in Georgia, insisted on her graduating from Clark College, which she did in 1948. Shortly thereafter, the couple were married and moved into a house on Seeley Road in Upper Deerfield.

Samah Pearson was one of hundreds of men hired in the West Indies, primarily from Jamaica, Barbados, the Bahamas and Trinidad-Tobago, beginning in about 1941. The Caribbean islands were initially open to large-scale recruiting by Seabrook Farms because of the Lend-Lease Act signed into law in March of that year. The main purpose of the law, drafted by President Roosevelt at the urging of British Prime Minister Winston Churchill, was to permit the United States, then bound (some would say strangled) by the Neutrality and Debt-Default Acts, to supply Great Britain and some other countries, notably the Soviet Union, with the materiel needed to defend against Nazi Germany. The simply stated concept, which Congress eventually bought, was that America was lending a neighbor (e.g., Great Britain) a hose (destroyers, etc.) with which that neighbor could put out a fire (Hitler's conflagration); if the hose became damaged through use, the neighbor would repay the lender in kind rather than with hard cash. Terms of repayment, in the language of the Act, were to be determined "as the President deems satisfactory."[18]

Although never stated in specific terms, repayment, or at least a quid pro quo, evidently included Great Britain's permission for American companies to recruit, through the War Manpower Commission, workers in any islands of the West Indies controlled or governed by Great Britain. Seabrook Farms, among others, took full advantage. However, although the Commission was content to round up men in Kingston, the capital of Jamaica, Jack Seabrook, who had previously visited the island, knew that the workers he wanted were not in the city but in the surrounding countryside. With the blessing and assistance of resident Episcopal Bishop R. O. C. King, Jack set up parish recruiting centers that not only attracted men accustomed to working in the fields, but also provided local doctors to screen out any unhealthy men. One of the reasons Jack said he moved his recruiting effort out of Kingston was that many city residents were on drugs.

At age thirty, Vivian Townsend set sail from Jamaica in 1943, landed at New Orleans, and then boarded a train for Seabrook. He arrived at Husted Station, which at the time was a busy depot less than five miles from Farm Center. (Many workers passed through this station, arriving for work at Seabrook and then leaving to go back home. Husted was also a receiving and shipping depot for some of Seabrook's products. The station is no longer there and neither are the tracks.) A Seabrook truck picked up Townsend at the station and drove him to a barracks at the so-called Mixner Division of Seabrook Farms, located on the border of Upper Deerfield and Hopewell Townships, an area that may have included the old truck farm where C. F. and his father started out. At the time, Seabrook Farms constituted nine divisions, each including a fixed amount of acreage and operating under a supervisor answerable to Jack Seabrook, then head of the overall farming operation. Almost all the men from the West Indies who worked in the fields either were single or had left their wives at home in the islands as per instructions from the Seabrooks. They arrived with only the clothes they were wearing when they left the dock in Kingston, Bridgetown, or Nassau, and one change. Most of the men later purchased clothes in the company store or in nearby towns.

Townsend worked in the fields until he took advantage of an opening in the freezing plant; eventually he became a foreman and stayed with Seabrook Farms until 1970, when he retired at age sixty-five. In 1943, Townsend and other field hands earned fifty cents an hour and worked sixty or seventy-two hours a week. "It was hard work for little pay," he said, "but it was a job." Later, as a foreman in the plant, he earned $2.33 an hour, working two weeks on day shift and then two weeks at night. During that time Seabrook maintained a savings account for each man, into which it deposited one dollar a day. Most men had their savings sent home to their families.

> When I first got to the plant, I worked along with Germans, Poles, Estonians, and Japanese Americans. I also remember a Russian who had been in the Russian Army in World War II. He was a foreman, but he couldn't read or write Russian let alone English. They [Seabrook management] asked us to be especially nice to the Japanese Americans when they came because, you know, it was still during the war. Later, I became very good friends with a Japanese American; in fact, I think he still lives over in the next town, but to tell you the truth I can't now remember his name.

Townsend was ninety-five years old when he was interviewed:

> I don't think I ever felt discrimination. Everybody liked us and we liked everybody.

Townsend married in 1947 and moved into a small house in Deerfield the next year. They were still living there in the summer of 2000.

Although Townsend may not have felt discrimination at Seabrook Farms—people said management would not allow it—prejudice was sometimes encountered in those days by both the transplants from the West Indies and African American workers when they ventured outside the global village into the provincial countryside, which lay below the Mason-Dixon Line, if that boundary is extended east from the Delaware River. Eula Johnson Pearson told about the time her Jamaican husband, Samah, went to a movie theater in Elmer, a small farming community north of Seabrook Farms in eastern Salem County. Shortly after he sat down, somebody called out in the dark, "There's a fly in the buttermilk."

Delroy Carey, who came to Seabrook from Jamaica by way of Florida, vividly portrays the difference between life in the global village, where multiracial and multicultural families lived and worked together as a community, and much of the world around them as it existed in the 1940s and 1950s. If, for example, a white Southern foreman or forelady exhibited prejudice toward a black worker, he said, management would handle the situation quickly. "You could always talk to Mr. Scheffer [the tough-acting, gruff-talking Hungarian], either in the plant or in his office. If you had a complaint against one of those [people], he'd take care of it. He was a gentleman all the way. If you were right, you were right, regardless of creed or color; if you were wrong, you were wrong."

Beyond the protection of Seabrook management, however, a person could be wrong simply because he or she was of a color other than white.

> We had a black dentist come down twice a month to our camp [to examine workers]; he was an army captain who had been wounded in the war. One time we wanted to do something special for him, so two of us took him to a diner in Bridgeton. We sat down, and the waitress served everyone else but passed us by, so we finally asked, "Can we get service here?" The waitress said, "We don't serve your kind here." We decided to go elsewhere and went outside, where we met a cop. He was a light-colored black man, and I guess they [the diner management] thought he was white. He took us back inside and said to the waitress, "Why don't you serve these people?" And she said, "Well, I have my orders." Then the owner came out and said he had a policy, but he finally agreed to serve us. At that point, the captain said, "Thanks very much, but I don't think I could eat your food," so we left and went to another restaurant and had no problem.

Many of the men from the West Indies became American citizens, married, raised families in the area, and continued to work for Seabrook Farms as permanent and valued employees. Delroy Carey, who still boasts that he was more literate when he came to this country than some native-born Americans who were his first bosses, is even prouder that when Seabrook Farms finally closed in 1982, he was the one with the key to the plant. "I locked up at the end. They took my picture."

Chapter 4

"Let's Go to New Jersey"

It was the week after Christmas, 1943, and George Sakamoto, age twenty-eight, was sitting in the smoking car of a New York Central train speeding east from Chicago. Some of his fellow passengers puffing their way to New York were young Caucasian soldiers and sailors on leave from Army and Navy bases heading home to family and friends. Sakamoto was on leave too, from Amache Relocation Center in Granada, Colorado, and heading a continent away from the home in Newcastle, California that he was forcibly prevented from returning to.

Sakamoto, his wife, Rose, and infant daughter, Barbara, were among 110,000 Japanese Americans who had been evacuated on short notice from the West Coast in the panicky months after the

Japanese attack on Pearl Harbor. He remembered, still with bitterness and resentment, the notices that were tacked to telephone poles and fence posts everywhere—from Bellingham, at the top of Washington State, down the Pacific Coast to San Diego, at the bottom of California: "All persons of Japanese ancestry, both alien and non-alien, will be evacuated from the above designated area effective. . . ."

Now, almost two years later, Sakamoto and a relatively small number of other Japanese American men had been granted permission by the War Relocation Authority (WRA) and the FBI, who no longer considered them an immediate threat to national security, to travel beyond the tar paper barracks and barbed wire of the ten relocation centers and search for employment on the East Coast. Each man had been given twenty-five dollars and a one-way train ticket, the first compensation from a government that, some Japanese Americans would say, had conspired with their Caucasian neighbors to steal their houses and profitable farms and vineyards.[1]

As the train snaked down the Appalachians and raced the last lap toward Forty-second Street, Sakamoto picked up the January 1944 issue of *Reader's Digest* someone had left behind and began leafing through it. This man who had known only farming since he was old enough to pick strawberries and grapes alongside his father stopped at page 95 when a headline caught his eye: "Assembly-Line Farmer." The farmer referred to was C. F. Seabrook, "the head of the world's largest truck-farming enterprise." Sakamoto read on:

> During peak months, Seabrook Farms and the packing plant employ as many as 7,500 workers, working under a closed shop agreement with the AFL. This makes Seabrook the first big farm to unionize in this country. The Seabrooks also have group life and hospital insurance plans, and their own school for the children of workers. Permanent workers are housed in modernized farmhouses, at rentals of from $4 to $17 a month. Big new glass-and-stone dormitories, each unit housing 750,

> are under construction for the migratory workers. These quarters will be rent free.[2]

When Sakamoto arrived in New York, he went directly to the local WRA office to inquire about Seabrook Farms. No one there had heard of Seabrook, but suggested he go on to Philadelphia and ask officials at the WRA office there. He took the next train south out of Penn Station. Seabrook Farms didn't ring a bell in the City of Brotherly Love either, but at least the WRA staff knew generally where to find the "flat, sandy stretches of southern New Jersey" described in the magazine article. Furthermore, these government bureaucrats also wanted to see this place in their virtual backyard that no less an authority than *Reader's Digest* called "probably the most highly mechanized farms in the country." So someone from the WRA office boarded a bus with Sakamoto, and together they made their way south to Bridgeton, the county seat of rural Cumberland County.

Sakamoto must have been awestruck when he arrived at Seabrook Farms. He and his wife had been deported from their thirty-acre farm north of Sacramento, and now he was confronted by thousands of acres of vegetables and fruit orchards, spread out in all directions as far as he could see. It was love at first sight. Besides, Sakamoto would soon run out of that twenty-five-dollar advance from the government and he needed a job. Of course, that's why the WRA allowed him to leave Amache in the first place.

The Seabrooks put him to work right away, repacking previously frozen products for sale to retail stores. It was a typical winter task. When he wasn't working, Sakamoto looked over the living arrangements and the surrounding community so that when he and his family were released officially from the relocation camp, he would know where they might call home, do their shopping, and send Barbara to school.

Sakamoto stayed until March or April. Before he went back to Amache, C. F., obviously pleased with his work, suggested that Sakamoto promote Seabrook Farms to other men in the camp, which he did. He returned to Seabrook in a month or two, still without his family, and was hired more or less permanently. That September, Rose's father died at the Tule Lake Relocation and

Segregation Center. He and many other issei (first-generation Japanese Americans still considered aliens by the government and never granted citizenship) had been kept at this camp in the northeast corner of California near the Oregon border under conditions more severe than those at most of the other camps. Many detainees then and later likened Tule Lake to a concentration camp.

Tule Lake was called a segregation center because a number of the Japanese Americans, particularly males, who were imprisoned there in 1944 were considered troublemakers or security risks by the government. Furthermore, many issei had answered no to Questions 27 and 28 on the Statement of United States Citizenship of Japanese Ancestry. Question 27 asked whether they would agree to serve in the United States armed services, and Question 28 asked them to swear "unqualified allegiance to the United States" and "defend the United States from any and all attack." The reason issei individuals in particular answered no to both questions was that the American government had never granted them U.S. citizenship and had always treated them as aliens—in effect, as citizens of Japan. If they answered yes, according to their logic, they would renounce their Japanese citizenship and be men and women without a country. Most of those who answered no to these questions were confined to Tule Lake, Rose's father among them.[3]

Sakamoto returned to Amache, where he joined Rose and Barbara, and together they went by train to attend her father's funeral. On the way back, he dropped off Rose and Barbara at Amache (he wanted to be secure in his job before bringing them to New Jersey), but joined his brother, James, for the trip back to Seabrook. When the brothers got off the train in Philadelphia, they walked into the teeth of a hurricane that was whipping up the coast. "We thought we would drown," Sakamoto recalled. "We got soaking wet walking from the Broad Street [train] station to a bus station at Thirteenth and Filbert. Anyway, we came to Seabrook [and] everything was at a standstill because of the hurricane . . . nothing moved here for about a week. . . . [Then] I got a job for my brother, and we went to work."

George Sakamoto, who didn't bring his family to Seabrook until 1945, was the first of more than 2,500 Japanese Americans from 600-plus families who came to work for the "world's largest truck-farming enterprise" in 1944 and 1945. The stories of how they got there from the relocation camps are almost as varied as the 100 species of chrysanthemum, the insignia of Japan's royal family.

Because of their experience with George Sakamoto, and in view of their many contacts in Washington, the Seabrooks had to be aware by the winter of 1943–1944 that the WRA and the American government in general were beginning to relax the Japanese American containment policy. Yet Jack Seabrook maintains that it didn't dawn on the company that it might be able to bring to its plants and fields great numbers of Japanese Americans until he walked into the offices of the Society of Friends in Philadelphia one bright, cold day shortly after Sakamoto first arrived on the scene.

Seabrook initially went to the Friends seeking their help in another matter: recruiting local African Americans. He thought the Society might run interference for Seabrook Farms in approaching the Philadelphia chapters of the Urban League and the NAACP. Instead of offering its help in that regard, the Society suggested it could be instrumental in putting the Seabrooks in touch with the right WRA officials, who in turn might open the gates to the relocation camps and allow the inmates to emigrate to South Jersey and jobs at Seabrook.

From the beginning of the evacuation and relocation of Japanese Americans, the Quakers had denounced the policy and had made every possible effort to have Japanese American families released back into a free society. Michi Nishiura Weglyn, who worked at Seabrook Farms along with her sister, later wrote "[The Friends are] warmly remembered to this day by all Japanese Americans. Where there was a camp, the Quakers made their presence felt, many driving the long, hot miles to even the most out-of-sight concentration camps to bring gifts, camp needs, and the precious reassurance that there were white Americans who cared." The American Friends Service Committee in Philadelphia had two persons working full-time on the resettlement of Japanese Americans. The Service Committee found housing for many Japanese American men and women. Those who were young and single were placed in hostels; families were located primarily in urban housing, perhaps because it was thought that Japanese Americans would be more easily absorbed into a city's population mix than into a country setting, where they might be as conspicuous as a "cool cat" wearing a 1940s zoot suit to a barn dance.[4]

When Jack Seabrook spoke with the Committee, both it and the WRA were leaning toward resettlement in rural areas, as this passage of a letter from a WRA official to the Committee indicates:

> As you know, most of the relocators to date have directed themselves toward the large metropolitan areas where most of them [Japanese American families] have obtained satisfactory acceptance and made good adjustments. However, the time is approaching when most of the people who are capable of adjusting themselves to city life will have left the center[s] and those who remain will be, by virtue of their past experiences in occupational backgrounds and their family compositions, unsuited for life in urban communities. Consequently, as time goes on, it is becoming urgent to find suitable relocation opportunities for family groups in rural areas.[5]

The bureaucratic phrase "experiences in occupational backgrounds" in translation means that many of the Japanese American families, like the Sakamotos, had been farmers or worked in produce markets prior to their evacuation.

Jack Seabrook first broached the idea of recruiting Japanese Americans in earnest with General Hugh D. Drum, then commander of the Eastern Defense Command, to determine whether the Army at the eastern end of the continent had any objections to Japanese Americans settling in South Jersey. Drum, who was no stranger to the Seabrooks, gave his okay. Then the family held council and decided to proceed cautiously. For one thing, regardless of how many families might come, new housing would be needed. Plans for building permanent cinder block apartments were set into motion. The family also concluded that it might be wise to first bring a small delegation of Japanese Americans to

Seabrook Farms and dazzle them with the vastness of the operation and the promise of jobs to any and all comers. The logic went like this: The delegation would be pleased with what they saw and heard, then return to camp and persuade fellow inmates to pack their bags and entrain for Philadelphia. If the plan worked at one camp, the Seabrooks reasoned, it could work at all ten camps. Seabrook recruiters could make the rounds and say, in effect, "Your brothers and sisters at Camp A have seen the light; they're already on their way to good jobs, decent housing and excellent schooling for their children." Of course, the flow of workers out of the camps, once the spigots were turned on, might in the long run inundate Seabrook Farms, but that was a risk the family was willing to assume.

In spring 1944, no one could envision an end to the tremendous demands for fruits and vegetables the U.S. armed forces and the free world's population had placed on Seabrook Farms: 60 million pounds in 1943, and the numbers were growing steadily. During the peak growing months, 7,500 employees worked 'round the clock seven days a week, and the need for more workers, particularly in the processing and packing plants, was still acute.

The call from Seabrook Farms finally went cross-country to the Jerome Relocation Center in the southeastern corner of Arkansas, roughly twenty miles west of the Mississippi and fifty miles north of the Louisiana border. The camp was located in the middle of swampland indigenous to the four most deadly snakes in America. The Army attempted to control the plague of omnipresent mosquitoes with DDT. The WRA concluded that no sane inmate would brave the surrounding muck and snakes, so it rarely placed guards in the towers, and the barbed wire fence probably could have been scaled fairly easily by the foolhardy. Jerome was considered by the WRA to be mostly free of troublemakers and recalcitrants. Furthermore, it was scheduled to begin phasing out in June 1944, the first of the camps to do so, which is probably why Jerome was chosen as the camp from which a delegation of three persons would be selected. At the request of Seabrook Farms, WRA officials chose Ellen Noguchi, Fuju Sasaki, and Harold Ouchida. It isn't clear why Ouchida was picked, but Noguchi and Sasaki had standing in the Jerome community. Noguchi, at twenty-four the youngest of the trio, was editor of the camp newsletter and had recently been selected by the camp director to be a member of the camp's Relocation Planning Commission. Sasaki went by the title of "Mayor," an honorific bestowed on him by fellow inmates who looked to him for leadership.

The delegation arrived at Seabrook Farms in April 1944, at about the same time that George Sakamoto was returning to Amache after his first three months of employment. The Seabrooks' hope to impress the visitors was more than fulfilled by Noguchi's reaction. Not only was she pleased by what she saw and heard, this became the "turning point" in her life: "When we got to Seabrook [Farms], Mr. [C. F.] Seabrook made every effort to see that we were well taken care of," she said. "He just made certain that we met the right people, like the mayor and the superintendent of schools [for Upper Deerfield], the principal of our Seabrook school, which was called the Moore School, and the people at the plant and the office, and [C. F.] also gave us a [paper] tour of the housing accommodations that were promised at the time [still on the drawing board]. After seeing Seabrook for ten days, I could hardly wait to get back."

Upon their return to the Jerome camp, the delegation discovered that Noguchi's unqualified enthusiasm did not rub off on as many fellow internees as they had anticipated. After meeting with families in both small and large groups, Noguchi and her two male companions thought a large number of them would be convinced that they should leave camp, travel half-way across the country, and settle in a place they had never heard of on a coast that was nearly as foreign to most of them as, say, the Mediterranean shore. What surprised them was the so-called prisoner mentality. The people they were speaking to had, like themselves, been interned for two years, first at assembly locations in California and then at Jerome. Even though they were surrounded by barbed wire and watch towers, they felt secure, and were afraid to face an uncertain life and to risk further discrimination.

Noguchi, whose fire for Seabrook Farms refused to be extinguished by the trepidation of fellow inmates, took two bold steps in succession. First, she accepted a marriage proposal from Kiyomi Nakamura, who had been part owner of a farm near Fresno and had offered his hand and his love several months earlier. Second— and not many brides-to-be, especially of Japanese ancestry, would have the temerity to pull it off—she issued something of an ultimatum along with her acceptance: "I told him, 'Okay. Now, let's go to New Jersey!'" They were married May 27, a little more than a month after Ellen's seeing New Jersey and Seabrook Farms for the very first time, and soon thereafter they headed east.

Coincidentally with the hard sell for Seabrook Farms at Jerome, George Sakamoto was apparently making his pitch at Amache. The camp newspaper carried a glowing article about Seabrook Farms; however, it mistakenly stated that jobs were being offered to Amache inmates only. By late spring, about the time the newlyweds were arriving in Bridgeton, and into the summer, recruitment of Japanese Americans moved into high gear. Seabrook Farms recruiters began showing up at one relocation camp after another. A Seabrook representative who traveled to the Rohwer Relocation Center, also in Arkansas, talked of the need for 240 women as cannery workers and 150 men as welders, sheet metal workers, electricians, pipe fitters, truck drivers, and general laborers. The camp newspaper at the Topaz Relocation Center in Utah reported that Seabrook Farms was offering jobs to men and women with no experience. Charles Nagao, who was interned at Manzanar Relocation Center in the California desert east of the Sierra Nevada, remembered his wife being interviewed by a Seabrook recruiter who showed her "beautiful, enticing brochures," evidently put together very quickly, that touted the virtues of working in the country.[6]

Although Seabrook Farms brochures may have been enticing, the reality of Japanese Americans coming to work at Seabrook Farms did not please everyone. L. H. Bennett, a project director for the WRA in Philadelphia, was one who wasn't completely sold on Seabrook Farms, perhaps because, by summer 1944, he was getting complaints from some Japanese American workers there. In a July 21, 1944 letter to William Huss at the Gila River Relocation Center, he wrote, "There are about 400 issei and nisei now in Philadelphia and quite a few in Seabrook; I would say around 100 in that one place," he wrote to the Gila River Relocation Center in Arizona at the end of July. "Of course, I am not too fond of the idea of Seabrook, and I do know that there are some of the issei who are working there who aren't happy about it." Bennett did not elaborate on the complaints, but the work schedule and pay were probably the primary causes for grumbling.

Shifts of eleven or twelve hours a day in a six-day workweek were not uncommon during peak periods. Most of the Japanese American men and women were hired to work on the processing and packaging lines, and it was monotonous work at best; the men in particular could become bored and irritable. When George Sakamoto first arrived at Seabrook Farms, he was paid forty-nine cents an hour, but was promised a raise and union membership within a month. When it didn't happen, he complained to C. F. himself and got the raise. Wages often depended on the job or, sometimes, as in the case of Sakamoto, whom you knew. Women workers generally were paid five cents less than men for the same work, which was not unusual for that time. When Japanese Americans agreed to come to Seabrook Farms, they pledged to work there for at least three months. No record can be found that tells how many of the 2,500 Japanese Americans who came to Seabrook left after three months, but in the summer of 1944, those who left either went back to camp or looked for work in metropolitan areas in the Midwest and the East, sometimes in defense plants where the pay was better and the hours not quite so long. They were still personae non grata in the West Coast locations they once called hometowns.

A letter in August from Bob Fort of the American Friends Service Committee to William Huss at Gila River Relocation Center, who had heard from Bennett a month earlier, was more upbeat about Seabrook Farms. He reported that Ellen Nakamura, who, in the two months since arriving with her husband had moved up and become assistant to the personnel director at Seabrook Farms, thought Seabrook was an especially good location for issei resettlement due to the fact that they could learn a new type of farming and have security, housing, and jobs. Nakamura and another Seabrook official also felt that the future of the issei and nisei (second generation) would be much better on the farms than in the canneries.

If Bennett had his reservations about Seabrook, the WRA evidently did not. By August 1944 the number of Japanese Americans transplanted from relocation centers to Seabrook Farms had increased to almost 300. One of them was James Mitsui, who came from the Jerome camp shortly after Ellen Noguchi Nakamura, although he didn't know her. Mitsui and his wife, Shigeyo, and two daughters had originally been held at the Tule Lake camp. They were transferred to Jerome when Tule Lake was turned into an internment camp for those Japanese Americans who had been labeled "disloyal" by the government because they had answered no to the so-called loyalty questions devised by the WRA. Mitsui decided to go to Seabrook Farms in response to a company representative's promotional pitch, but also because of an echo from his past. "When I was a kid [back in California] I went to work and helped make boxes [for fruit], and this elderly issei called two or three of us kids over to him. He said, 'You know, young kids like you should live on a farm. Go east.' I think what he meant was that [since] the fruit we raised we shipped to eastern markets and had to pay the railroad fare, why not go to where the markets are."

Like a number of men with families, Mitsui decided to go to Seabrook alone on a trial basis. "I wanted to establish myself first. Let me tell you, it wasn't easy leaving family." He traveled with five other men from the camp, all of them strangers to him. He had no seat reservation on the train, and it was crowded with servicemen, as most trains were at the time. "I didn't have a place to sit; I just kept walking around. Finally, there were two seats open. One had an Army jacket on it and one didn't. I was so tired, I slept there for a couple of hours. I knew they were soldiers' seats, so when I woke up, I left, [and] the rest of the time I didn't have a seat."

Upon arrival in Philadelphia, Mitsui checked into a hotel and contacted Seabrook Farms. He was told to stay put for a while because of an incident that had occurred in central New Jersey (a Japanese American family working on a farm had been threatened by people in the area). After a week he took the bus to Bridgeton and showed up at the Seabrook Farms personnel office. He was scheduled to work the next day, Saturday, but he asked if he could start on Monday so he could look around and get accustomed to the place. His request was granted, and he left the personnel office on his way to the housing office to be assigned to the dormitory for single men. As he walked along the side of the road, a young man in a car passed him and yelled, "Go back home, you Jap." Of course, he was home. It was the only time in the months and years that followed that he ever felt any animosity.

Although the Japanese Americans were the first Asians to be included in the workforce at Seabrook Farms, they joined a global village in the making. Already in the mix were Italians, Jamaicans and others from the West Indies, workers from Tennessee, coal miners from West Virginia, local African Americans, and a few Russians, Poles, and Dutch people. In addition, at about the same time Ellen Noguchi Nakamura arrived on the scene, so did a contingent of German prisoners of war (POWs), part of the famed Deutsches Afrika Korps (DAK). They were housed at a nearby Civilian Conservation Corps camp that had been abandoned at the start of the war.

They may have been men of the DAK Assault Group, which was the last German unit to surrender to the allies in North Africa on May 12, 1943, when their commander signaled the Americans that the "Afrika Korps had fought itself to the condition where it can fight no more."[7] At Seabrook, the POWs worked alongside everyone else, but other workers, particularly women, were cautioned not to fraternize with them. However, Helen Cubberley, who worked at Seabrook Farms in the summer of 1944 as a quality grader for the State of New Jersey, found it nearly impossible not to communicate with POWs who were working on the same platform where farmers were unloading their produce for her inspection. "One day, one of them indicated to me that he would like to have a mirror. Living in a POW camp, I'm sure they didn't have many luxuries. The next day I gave him a small mirror from my purse. . . . Later, in appreciation, he gave me a bronze panther [*panzer*] he had made from a melted down belt buckle in the craft workshop. I never learned his name. One other POW was an artist and [painted] Ye Olde Centerton Inn [a fine restaurant dating to the 1700s that is close by the place where the POWs were once housed], which has hung for many years over the fireplace in the Inn."[8]

Robert Busnardo was a kid growing up in an Italian family in 1944; his immediate neighbors in the global village were Jamaicans. He remembers the German POWs digging ditches nearby for the installation of water pipes. "Their guards would tell us [kids] not to go near them, but of course we did. They [the prisoners] had chewing gum, and we didn't, so they would pitch out a five pack to us. I believe that half those guys, if they had turned them loose, would have kissed the ground they were on. They wanted to be Americans; I mean, you could just see it in their faces."

By the time the Japanese Americans arrived, therefore, working and living with persons of another nationality or race who spoke another language was not a novelty at Seabrook Farms. The fact that the Seabrooks introduced the Japanese Americans into the plants and farms gradually at first and took them around to meet other workers also helped alleviate any hard feelings.

Immediately prior to and during the emigration from the relocation centers, members of the Seabrook family, some community leaders, and local WRA officials spoke to civic groups in and around Bridgeton about the critical need for workers, how Japanese Americans could help meet that need, and why they were good people to have around. The *Bridgeton Evening News* often placed reports of these meetings on the front page and was supportive editorially. A front-page article reported a speech by Harold S. Fistere of the WRA to the city's Board of Trade. Fistere pointed out that the vast majority of Japanese Americans had been incarcerated "through no fault of their own" and that their release from the relocation centers and employment at places like Seabrook Farms would "aid the war effort." He ended by referring to the Japanese Americans as "valuable farm workers," many of whom had owned or worked on farms in California.[9]

John Melchiorre, who worked in a management position at Seabrook Farms after his discharge from the Army in 1945, believes the schools were instrumental in promoting good feelings toward Japanese Americans, or at least in ameliorating any ill will or misunderstanding. Principals and teachers prepared students for the arrival of Japanese American children, who joined the already interesting mix of race and national origins reflecting the potpourri at Seabrook Farms, where most of the children's parents worked. In addition, teachers and students—and through them, parents and the community at large—discovered that many Japanese American children were very smart, sometimes ahead of their Caucasian peers (a fact still noted today when SAT scores are reported).

The relocation centers made every effort to allow children and youths to continue their education. John Fuyuume, who first came to Seabrook Farms as a summer worker sorting lima beans and peas, remembers how the Gila Relocation Center in Arizona converted a block of barracks into a school for kindergarten through grade twelve. Some of the teachers were internees, and others were hired by the WRA from nearby communities. Fuyuume completed his last year of high school there. "My favorite teacher was Miss Mabel Sheldon, who had been a Methodist missionary to India, but was unable to return to New Delhi because of the war," he remembered. "She taught English at our camp, and Miss Montgomery, from Tucson, was my biology teacher. I remember those two teachers very well. I don't recall the name of my civics teacher because he gave me a B; [otherwise] I was a straight A student." Fuyuume's diploma was issued by Butte High School, the name given to the camp school. Through the American Friends Service Committee he earned a scholarship to the Eastman School of Music at the University of Rochester (and a ticket out of the camp). He remains a virtuoso pianist today. When the Fuyuume family was ordered to leave their home on short notice in 1942, John's grand piano was left behind in the care of his first piano teacher. Long after the war, when his teacher died, her will left—returned—the piano to her former pupil.

In April 1945, when most of the 2,500 Japanese Americans had arrived at Seabrook Farms and while young Americans were dying by the hundreds every day on Okinawa, Leonard Goodis, a Bridgeton High School senior, stood in front of the Kiwanis Club to talk about tolerance. He had been invited to speak about the "Japanese American Problem," but he dismissed the assigned topic by telling his audience that there was no problem. Goodis concluded his remarks: "In the final analysis . . . prejudice can never be legislated away. Each one of us will have to eliminate our own small touch of it. Over and above the moral indictment against it, prejudice must go if civilization is to remain. We in Bridgeton have been given an opportunity to deal prejudice a telling blow. We can be proud of our use of that opportunity."[10]

Too bad Goodis did not have the ear of Peruvian and American officialdom in 1942 when the two governments conspired to heap injustice upon injustice on Peruvians of Japanese ancestry. Just as many historians believe the evacuation of Japanese Americans from our West Coast had more to do with prejudice and resentment over the economic and civic accomplishments of both issei and nisei than with the defense of America, the same undercurrents fueled the deportation of Peruvian Japanese. "As for persons of Japanese ancestry residing in the democratic republic of Peru," wrote Michi Nishiura Weglyn, "racial antagonism fed by resentment of the foreign element as being exceedingly successful economic competitors had more to do with the Peruvian Government's spirited cooperation [with the United States] than its concern for the defense of the Hemisphere. Racial feelings against the Japanese minority, abetted by the press, had burst into occasional mob action even before the Pearl Harbor attack."[11]

One of the victims was Rose Dodohara, of Lima, Peru, who was ten years old in 1942 when Peruvian police rounded up all issei who were suspected of exercising leadership or influence in the community. Dodohara attended a private school where children were taught the history of Japan and its culture and language in the morning, and Peruvian history and Spanish language in the afternoon. "The first thing that happened was that they arrested all the Japanese school teachers. They just disappeared." But the worst was yet to come. Her father and uncle, both local businessmen, were jailed temporarily. When he was released after a few weeks, her father went into hiding for fear he would be picked up again and separated from his family. "He found a chicken farmer [and stayed with him]. If anyone suspicious came to the farm, he would hide in the coop with the chickens." The authorities did come looking for him, but at the Dodohara home, not at the chicken farm. "The security people would come, sometimes in the middle of the night, and search all over the house, even under the beds."

Somehow, still lying low at the chicken farm, Rose's father heard that issei like himself and their families were going to be sent to an internment camp in America. "He said to us," she reported, 'If they want to ship us all together, that's fine. If they want to shoot us, we all die together.' So that's how we came to the United States"—not exactly how most aliens find their way to the land of the free and home of the brave.

The Dodohara family was assigned to the Crystal City Internment Camp southwest of San Antonio, about thirty miles from the Mexican border. Crystal City was different from the camps run by the WRA. Crystal City was one of eight facilities operated by the Justice Department and the only one of the Justice Department camps that allowed families. The others were reserved for single issei men who were suspected of being a threat. Families at Crystal City lived in small, detached two-room buildings; one room was the kitchen and the other was for living and sleeping. The buildings had no hot water, and families used outdoor, communal latrines. Children could attend either English- or Japanese-language schools from elementary grades through high school. The Dodoharas sent Rose to Japanese-language school because the rumor circulating in the camp was that everyone at Crystal City would be either deported to Japan outright or swapped for American civilians who had been caught unaware by the events of December 7 and 8 and were being detained in Japan or in areas under Japanese control.

The Dodoharas and the other families had good reason to fear deportation or exchange. From the beginning of the removal of Peruvian Japanese, the U.S. government considered them trading chips, particularly the issei men. That is why, when the relocation centers started to close in the latter part of 1944 and early 1945, the Peruvian Japanese were kept in the internment camps until the end of the war in the summer of 1945. Even then, for many of the Peruvian Japanese the cruelest part of the ordeal was yet to come.

The Peruvian government refused to allow any Japanese to return to their homes in that country. The U.S. Justice Department, in a stroke of convoluted logic, decided that these people whom the United States had helped to kidnap from their homes and jobs in Peru now "lacked proper credentials; they had entered the U.S. illegally, without visas and passports." Thus caught between hard alternatives, some 700 men and their dependents volunteered to be sent to a defeated, pulverized Japan. The U.S. government was ready to oblige this sacrifice when Wayne Collins, a San Francisco attorney who became a hero to both Peruvian Japanese and Japanese Americans, went to court to prevent this gross miscarriage of justice imposed on innocent people by the Justice Department. Collins was successful in stopping the removal program, and by summer 1946, a year after the war's end, the families held in the internment camps, including Crystal City, were placed in "relaxed internment" and released.[12] Not quite free, and with a stigma like house arrest still hanging over them, the Dodoharas and a number of other families embarked for New Jersey and Seabrook Farms.

Rarely did Japanese Americans travel to Seabrook in groups large enough to fill a train coach. Many came with small groups of friends, in couples, or alone. In some cases older children in their teens or twenties arrived a year or two after their parents because they left the camp ahead of the family to go to college or to take a job, usually in a city. The ride east was particularly vivid and memorable for one small child: "In August 1945, I remember coming to Seabrook on a hot, dusty train from Poston, Arizona [where the internment camp was located]. The shades were pulled down, [but] we peeked out because my grandmother told us there were Indians watching us. On that day memory and imagination mixed, and I could swear there were Indians with lances sitting on their horses peering at us on our click-clacking train."[13]

For Chieko Furushima, née Segimoto, the story that ended happily at Seabrook Farms began frighteningly, immediately after the attack on Pearl Harbor. The Segimotos, mother and father and four children, lived on Terminal Island, a finger of land that juts into San Pedro Bay and is attached to the same body of land as the naval shipyard at Long Beach, California. Her father fished for the cannery on the island, and her mother worked in the packing house; Chieko had recently graduated from high school, which was on the mainland. On December 7, 1941, Segimoto was out at sea fishing. Before he could return to port, he was plucked from his boat by American naval authorities and eventually housed, along with other "enemy aliens," in the Justice Department's Fort Lincoln Internment Camp in North Dakota. The family who had kissed husband and father good-bye one morning before the war never saw him again until after the war, nearly four years later. Mother and four daughters, together with all other Japanese Americans left on Terminal Island, were given notice in February 1942 that they had forty-eight hours to get off the island. Most of the families lived in housing rented from the owners of the cannery, but they had to leave behind all of their own furniture and appliances. The government offered no housing alternatives on the mainland; all were left to fend for themselves. Some families lived for a time in private Japanese schools (before they closed). Fortunately, the Segimotos had cousins in the area, with whom they stayed until the general roundup of Japanese Americans on the West Coast, when they were shipped to Manzanar Relocation Center.

Chieko left the camp in May 1945, one of a dozen young men and women who took advantage of the lenient leave policy then in force to go in search of jobs in the Chicago area. A girlfriend who had preceded her to the city suggested that she take a position as a domestic, which she did. Her mother and sisters remained in camp because they, like a number of others who feared discrimination and reprisals from fellow Americans on the other side of the barbed wire, felt secure behind the fence. Chieko remained with the Chicago family until 1946. By then her own family had left camp and moved to Seabrook, where one sister worked for C. F. and his wife as a domestic in the Big House on Polk Avenue. "I came out to visit them. I never left," Chieko said.

Life at Seabrook was, in some important ways, harsher for the latecomers than it was for those Japanese Americans who arrived in 1944. The problem was that the Seabrooks, although they were more than pleased to get additional workers, had not counted on getting so many so quickly. By late 1945 and into 1946, Seabrook Farms had run out of government-funded housing in Hoover Village and had hastily constructed Hoover Village Annex. Esther Ono, who was nineteen in the fall of 1945, vividly remembers detraining at Philadelphia in the company of other Japanese American families and then being herded into a Seabrook tractor trailer that was poorly ventilated and had wooden benches along both sides. The families' luggage was dumped in the middle of the van, "I had been looking forward to something nice, but when I got into that cattle car, I started to cry. My younger sister, who was eight, said, 'I think this truck stinks.'" When the truck unloaded its human cargo at Hoover Village Annex, Esther's disillusion was complete. "It was just like camp again—tar paper barracks."

Esther's sister was disgusted by the smells of the trailer, but there were worse odors to come. Theresa Masatani, née Mukoyama, was among the Peruvian Japanese who arrived at

Seabrook Farms from the Crystal City camp in Texas and were also housed at the Annex. The Annex went up so fast that some toilets had not yet been connected to the sewer system, and so a ditch outside the barracks often contained raw sewage. On Halloween night Theresa's brother, along with some friends, was fooling around on a little bridge that spanned the ditch; he slipped off and landed in the muck. "He came out covered in turds," Esther reported. But conditions improved quickly. "The barbed wire and soldiers were missing. At least we had freedom," she said.

Iddy Taniguchi Asada recalls her first look, as a young girl, at the strange place called Seabrook Farms almost 3,000 miles from her home in California: "When we passed in front of the plant [at night], we were awed at the brightness of the front platform ablaze in lights like an amusement center. We saw the working women, who wore little white caps, which were stiffly starched, and [were] attired in blue uniforms." Iddy and her family (mother, sister and brother) were dropped off at their sixteen- by forty-eight-foot barracks in Hoover Annex. "We were told to fill our bed ticking with the straw set aside for that purpose. After the mattresses were filled, we placed them on our double bunk beds and literally hit the hay. My mother, Suzie, and Jim were told to report to work in the plant the next day."[14]

John Seabrook, C. F.'s grandson and Jack's son, interviewed Esther Ono for an article he was writing. Esther, who now owns and operates a beauty parlor close by the spot where Hoover Annex once stood, which at the time reminded her of the internment camp she and her family had just left, told him, "I always felt grateful that Mr. Seabrook did undertake to do this for us." Her word of thanks caused Seabrook to sense "a familiar twist of sansei [third generation Japanese] cynicism. Yes, C. F. helped these people, but it was always good business to help them. With the Japanese Americans, Seabrook Farms got a group of amazingly loyal, uncomplaining, hardworking people, who had a lot to do with the company's great success after the war."[15]

They were all those things—and they had *gamon*. Translated from Japanese, the term means "fortitude, endurance." Those families fresh from the internment camps where they had been dumped by their own government still demonstrated, miraculously and fortunately, old-fashioned American grit.

Chapter 5

Beyond the Golden Door

I lift my lamp beside the golden door.

From *The New Colossus* by Emma Lazarus,
the poem inscribed on the Statue of Liberty

Sometime in the summer or fall of 1948, shortly after Congress passed the Displaced Persons Act that allowed 205,000 people in displaced persons (DP) camps in Germany to emigrate to this country,[1] the Reverend Herbert Dick, then pastor of St. John's

Lutheran Church in Bridgeton, called on C. F. at his Seabrook Farms office with a proposition. On the one hand, Seabrook Farms, as always in those banner years of round-the-clock production, needed workers even after the influx of Japanese Americans, and, on the other hand, thousands of European refugees, including hundreds of men and women from Estonia and the other Baltic nations, languished in DP camps and yearned to come to America and build a new life to replace what had been shattered by war. No one knows for certain, but Pastor Dick also probably told C. F., the seventh-grade dropout, that a number of the Estonians he could get for his operation were college educated and had had responsible positions in business, the professions, and government in their homeland. C. F. must have been delighted. The Old Man and his sons were always on the lookout for employees who listed higher education credentials on their resumes and thus might be expected to move up quickly into supervisory positions. Best of all, in the case of the Estonians, he could have workers of this caliber cheaply.

Naturally, C. F. said yes to the proposition. Seabrook Farms would eventually sponsor and offer home and work to more than 600 Estonian men, women, and children.

For most of them, the journey from Estonia to Seabrook Farms was fraught with delays, disappointments, and perils.

Estonians, Latvians, and Lithuanians biding their time in DP camps in 1948 had been on the run from their native lands since 1944, but they and their ancestors had actually been trying to avoid domination either by Russia or Germany for centuries. Imperial Russia ruled over the Baltic countries from the eighteenth century until World War I and the subsequent Bolshevik Revolution. Then, for a while, from 1918 to 1920, the Red Army on the east and units from the defeated German Army on the west, together with Baltic armies, contested for control of the three states. Finally, by the summer of 1920, Estonia, Latvia, and Lithuania became independent states. Yet their freedom was short-lived. A new German Army, this one more powerful and even more vicious than the remnants of the Kaiser's forces at the end of World War I, conquered their lands in short order in the early 1940s. Then, as the tide of war turned against Nazi Germany, the Red Army again rolled over the Baltic states.

Although life under the Nazis had not been pleasant, the Estonians and the other peoples had not suffered greatly. But they knew, from their collective memory, what to expect from the Russians: fierce repression at the very least, but certainly a reign of terror that could round up most of the nations' intelligentsia and leaders in every sector of society and condemn them to exile in Siberia or worse. Consequently, beginning in 1944, Estonians, Latvians, and Lithuanians began to flee their homes en masse. Some escaped to Finland and Sweden; many others fled to Germany, as they could often hitch a ride aboard a German troopship that was bringing home what was left of Hitler's army in that part of Europe.

When the bombs began to fall from Soviet planes in the fall of 1944, Eevi Truumees was nine years old and living with her grandmother, mother, and sister in a small town in Estonia southwest of the capital city of Tallinn. Her father, who had served in the Estonian government when it was independent, had gone into hiding when the Russians crossed the border. Together with many of their compatriots, the Truumees women commenced one of those perilous journeys, fleeing almost immediately to Parnu on the Baltic Sea. They carried two suitcases but left behind treasures and memorabilia gathered and stored for generations. In an interview, Eevi Truumees recalled: "We boarded one of the last [German troop] ships out of the harbor. We docked at Danzig, now in Poland but then in German hands, and the first thing off the boat we were sprayed with some kind of powder to kill the lice and whatever else we were carrying."

From Danzig, the Truumees family, along with Eevi's uncle, Albert Vilms, and his wife and three young sons, traveled by train to Berlin and a camp where they were served soup made of potato peels, carrot greens, and "whatever the German Army didn't eat." Berlin was not a good place to be in October 1944. "The bombardment was terrible," Truumees continued. "We got it from all sides—Russians, Americans, and British. I remember the Berlin zoo being bombed, and some of the lions and snakes were loose in the city. But, amazingly enough, I never remember being scared." Later, the Truumees and Vilms families, together with forty or so other Estonians, were taken by train to a small community in Czechoslovakia, fifty kilometers west of Prague. There, they were at first assigned one large room. The Truumees and Vilms families soon moved in with a German family, who not only did not welcome their presence but also tried to smoke them out of their half of the house by sticking rags in the chimney that served the stove used for cooking and heating.

The brave little band of Estonians—Albert Vilms was the only man and the others were women and very young children—remained in Czechoslovakia until May 5, 1945, three days before the end of the war. But the worst of the ordeal was just beginning. The Estonians and other refugees were now joined by Czechs and Germans in a mad dash to the west to escape the conquering Russian Army coming from the east and north. At first they traveled by freight train, but, living with constant fear that Russian troops would either stop the train or perhaps blow it up, they gave up traveling by rail and took to walking. "I remember we came into a village where Russian soldiers herded us into a fenced-in area," said Truumees. "Some people thought they were going to shoot us. [Instead] they started shooting Germans on the street right in front of us. Once they were finished with the killing, they piled bodies onto some kind of wagon and had some Germans who were still alive pull the dead people out of there."

The women and children and Albert Vilms walked—*walked*—more than 150 miles through the forest and up and over the Bohemian highlands into eastern Germany. From time to time they heard gunfire in the distance and assumed that hard-drinking Russian soldiers were still shooting Germans or anyone else who looked unfriendly or got in their way. Truumees recalled their journey vividly: "We slept in the woods. Sometimes we'd come across a vacant farmhouse and go inside looking for food. Or we'd dig up potatoes rotting in the ground and eat them."

At last they arrived in Jena, southwest of Leipzig. At the time, Jena was in a no-man's-land between Russian and American lines. At first, the Americans would not allow the group to cross from the Russian sector into their zone, probably because, as the war was ending, the occupying armies were beginning to adhere to the occupation zone drafted on maps by politicians during the war. Not to be thwarted after their long and arduous journey, the Estonians sneaked over the border through a wheat field, bending over so their heads stayed below the top of the grain. The Americans didn't send them back; instead, they housed the weary, scruffy group in old German barracks, twenty persons to a room with bunk beds. But within two or three weeks, the American army pulled out of the area and sent the Estonians and other refugees west in cattle cars.

At some point—Eevi Truumees doesn't recall where—the train stopped and the locomotive disengaged and left the cars on a siding. Again, the Estonians and other refugees were petrified, fearing that the Russians would catch up to them sitting out in the open. "So, my uncle and a few other men got together, and somehow, somewhere, they found a locomotive [and engineer] and we got going again." The train got as far as Augsburg, northwest of Munich, well inside the American occupation zone. Evidently, Russians had been living in German housing in Augsburg, because Russian soldiers had been assigned to round up any Russian citizens and take them back to the Russian zone. "Most of them were screaming that they didn't want to go back to Russia. Also, the Russians tried to persuade some of the Estonians to return to Estonia. The Americans had to place military police around the housing so the Russians wouldn't run off with us."

Eevi not only didn't go with the Russians, she didn't go anywhere for six years. Beginning in early 1949, a number of Estonians left for the port at Bremerhaven and then sailed the ocean to New York and Seabrook, but a quartet of females, one of them Eevi's seventy-year-old grandmother and two of them minor children, was not high on the list of displaced persons for whom American sponsors—including C. F.—were looking.

The exceedingly long wait experienced by the Truumees family was an exception, but delays in getting displaced persons resettled in America were common. One of the most trying aspects of the program for the sponsors was the length of time that elapsed between their submission of an assurance and the arrival of the sponsored alien. In its final report to the president and Congress in 1952, four years after passage of the Displaced Persons Act, the U.S. Displaced Persons Commission stated, "[The] processing of an applicant from the time the assurance was submitted to the emigrant's arrival involved an average of eight months in duration and much longer if any complications arose."[2] Naturally, whenever government bureaucrats are involved, complications are sure to follow. Thus, it was not unusual for the preliminary processing to take much longer than eight months. One of the worst consequences of the delay was that a displaced person might arrive after his or her services were most needed. "Many potential employers indicated they could use many displaced persons, provided they had some assurance that they could look forward to their arrival within a reasonably short period of time. Agricultural employment had seasonal peaks and it was important to have workers at particular periods if they were to be assured full-time jobs."[3] If, for example, most of the displaced persons Seabrook Farms sponsored arrived in late fall, the company would have found it difficult—nigh impossible—to put most of them to work until the following spring.

Preliminary processing included personal documentation, physical examination, and security investigation (to weed out Nazi collaborators and Communists). Moreover, by 1950 the U.S. government had sent teams of "occupational selectors" to Germany. The team whose task it was to screen potential farmworkers to ensure their suitability for agricultural employment consisted of county agents, farm extension workers, and farm specialists who spoke German.[4] For the Estonians headed to Seabrook Farms, this particular screening, which, in any event, commenced after many of them already had departed for America, was almost laughable. When asked by screeners what their previous agricultural experience had been in Estonia, few adults could afford to be completely honest because few had held any job that could be even generously construed as agricultural. Many of the Estonians came from urban areas and had been employed in business, industry, or the professions.

The Reverend Toomas Vaga, who was eleven years old when he came to Seabrook Farms with his family in May 1949, said displaced persons soon learned how to give correct responses to questions asked by interviewers. "One of the questions put to my mother was, 'Who's going to take care of your three children when you go to work in the plant?' You had to know what the correct answer was. Of course, an incorrect answer was that you'd leave them alone. Another incorrect answer was that you'd leave them in the nursery. Although, as it turned out, Seabrook had a nursery, most farm operations did not. In my mother's case, the correct answer was that her brother-in-law's wife, who also had an assurance to go to Seabrook, would take care of them."

The DP camps, such as the one where the Truumees resided for so long, were first operated by the United Nations Relief and Rehabilitation Administration (UNRRA). Later, the International Relief Organization (IRO) assumed management. However, Lutherans—and most Estonians belonged to that denomination—could also rely on the Lutheran Immigration and Refugee Service (LIRS). One of the first contacts anyone had with Lutheran refugees was in March 1946, when the World Council of Churches received a letter from eight Latvian pastors serving Lutherans from the Baltic countries who were confined to the DP camps: "We have been told that we shall soon be sent back if our country asks our return. We have no desire to go until our country once more gains its free government and has freedom of religion." One of the pastors later testified before officials of relief organizations headquartered in Geneva about Russian oppression in the Baltic states.[5]

The first displaced persons sponsored by the Lutheran Church to immigrate to the United States arrived at New York on October 30, 1948. Cordelia Cox, director of the Lutheran Resettlement Service, described the event: "It is an unforgettable sight to see families coming down the gangplank, being checked off a master list by a sponsoring organization, and taken to the correct place to wait for their baggage. They come with wonder and hope and fear in their faces, holding tightly to children, walking cautiously and hesitantly, immediately responsive to the smile and welcome of a person wearing an organization arm band waiting at the end of the gangplank."[6]

The following spring, the Lutheran Welfare Association of New Jersey notified Seabrook Farms that the first group of Estonians whom C. F. had agreed to employ as workers in his fields and plants and had promised to house and otherwise care for were on their way. In a letter dated March 23, 1949, and addressed to Harold Fistere, Seabrook's personnel director, the Association stated, "We are sending you . . . the list of the Displaced Persons who have been assigned to the jobs which you so kindly offered. We are listing the names, ages, sex and type of employment." The writer, Julie Matzinger, who apologized for the delay in sending the list, said the Association had had difficulty in determining "the sex of many of these people from the names given." Presumably, she meant that the Association could not decide, for example, whether Orm Aniline, age six, was male or female. Indeed, the column designating sex remained blank beside Orm's name on the list sent by the Association. Mrs. Matzinger guessed that Seabrook Farms would be sympathetic to the Association's problem: "I expect this kind of difficulty is not new for you in view of the many Japanese people whom you have had in your employ." She evidently assumed that Seabrook might have had difficulty in determining in advance the sex of, say, someone named Harumi Taniguchi (female).

Most of the adults on the list were designated as either vegetable processors or frozen food processors, although it appears that the Association was not sure as to what tasks some adults would or could perform for Seabrook Farms. For example, Gertrude Aniline, age thirty-eight, was slated to work as a vegetable processor (probably sorting vegetables on the assembly line), but no occupation was listed for Linda Baunis, age thirty-three. Ilmar Reinvald, age forty-seven, was tagged as a frozen food processor, but his wife Virve, age thirty-three, was assigned no task. (In 1951, Ilmar became one of five members of the newly formed Seabrook Estonian Association Council.) Occupations were not stated for any of the children, of course, but the families would discover that at Seabrook Farms, children aged twelve and older were expected to work in the fields, orchards, nursery, or bulb garden during summer recess.

Albert Vilms, Eevi Truumees's uncle, and his family embarked from Bremerhaven for America aboard the troop ship *General Haan* on May 3, 1949. He was a graduate of Tartu University and had practiced law in Viljandi; in 1939 he had been elected mayor. Yet that spring he was on his way to Seabrook Farms and a job as a common laborer. The ship docked in New York on the evening of May 13, and at ten o'clock the next day, Saturday, he and his wife, Else, and their three sons took their first steps on American soil. In his personal diary, as translated by his son Jaak in September 2001, Vilms wrote:

> The same day at 2:00 P.M. we departed New York for Seabrook [by Seabrook bus] where we arrived at 6:30.

Beyond the Golden Door

Our new home was Hoover Village, with its four rows of barracks. We were assigned the three-room, first-row barrack number 1033. In the middle of the first, larger room was a round iron stove, which burned coal briquets or wood. There was an electric range and a sink with a cold water tap. Communal showers and laundry facilities were located in separate barrack buildings, between the second and third rows of barracks. The toilets were also in those buildings. The barracks were clean; there was clean bedding on the beds, and every family received sets of white towels. There was a large coal bin outside against the front wall. The Seabrook Company provided free coal for heating that first winter.

Sunday morning the family had breakfast in the company cafeteria and then attended an English-language church service at Community House, conducted by the Reverend Dick, the person most responsible for their being at Seabrook. They sat in on an orientation program in the afternoon. The next day, Monday, at six o'clock in the evening, Albert joined the night shift in the packaging department. "I recall that I had to take full boxes from the end of the packing conveyor and put them on a cart. The boxes were not heavy, but they came so fast that I could not load them on the cart, and some fell on the floor. Seeing that I was not up to that job, they tried me out at a few other jobs. Finally, I ended up in cold storage. The first night I thought would be my first and last night in the Seabrook factory." Albert Vilms retired from Seabrook almost twenty-five years later, having worked most of that time as a shift foreman in the Prepared Foods Division. He was also the first president of the Seabrook Estonian Association Council.

The Vilms family had come from the Augsburg-Hochfeldt Displaced Persons Camp in Germany, the same camp where their relatives, the Truumees family, had remained. Eevi Truumees described the camp as "very nice housing." The DPs were not confined to barracks but were mostly living in homes confiscated from German families. The refugees may have been crowded and cramped in the available rooms, but Eevi could still proclaim

Augsburg "one of the best camps in all of Germany." Therefore, Seabrook's Hoover Village, a collection of sixty-six hastily built, prefabricated barracks, was an even greater shock to the Estonians than it had been for the Japanese Americans who preceded them. The Japanese Americans had been dismayed because Hoover Village reminded them of the internment camps they had just left. For Estonians from camps like Augsburg-Hochfeldt, Hoover Village was worse than the living quarters they had just vacated.

Alan Palmer, who was director of housing for Seabrook Farms during this period, witnessed the newcomers' reactions firsthand:

> The [barracks of Hoover Village], although spotlessly clean, were about as unattractive as they could be; set closely together without a blade of grass or a tree to soften their appearance, about the best that could be said for them was that they did provide a degree of shelter from the elements. The Estonians were totally unprepared for the type of housing to which they were taken; they had no idea that in wealthy America, which had not been ravaged by war, such housing could exist. The housing staff was equally unprepared for such a tearful reaction, and, although they could not understand the words in Estonian, the tones of angry disappointment transcended any language barrier. The first night spent in Seabrook by each group of new arrivals was a bitterly traumatic experience for everyone concerned.[7]

Like the Japanese Americans and other transplanted peoples before them, the Estonians and the few Latvians made the best of their situation. After all, Seabrook Farms "provided an opportunity for the newly arrived refugees to lay a groundwork for their new life in the United States. Soon, flowerbeds appeared in front of the barracks and vegetable gardens began to sprout nearby. Their sparse living quarters were soon furnished and decorated.

TV antennas began appearing on rooftops, and some even managed to purchase automobiles, both a necessity and a status symbol in their new homeland."[8]

Meanwhile, back at the Augsburg-Hochfeldt Displaced Persons Camp, the Truumees family was, at long last, getting ready to go to America. The time was September 1951, two and a half years after Uncle Albert and his family had departed.

Eevi's grandmother was unable to go to America by ship because her arthritis, aggravated by the arduous journey in 1944–45, prevented her from going up the gangplank. Therefore, Uncle Albert arranged for her to travel to New York by airplane. Eevi, her mother, and her sister stepped off the Seabrook bus in front of Hoover Village on September 25, exactly seven years since the three of them, along with Eevi's grandmother and the Vilms family had scrambled off the German troop ship at Danzig.

Years later, Eevi was asked by some American friends whether she and her family resented the rude housing, the long hours, the hard work and low pay. After all, they said, your mother had been a school principal and ended up sorting beans, and your uncle was a lawyer and mayor of a city, and his first job was on the bottom rung at the plant. "I answered no. We were grateful for the opportunity. It was a beginning, and as my grandmother used to say, 'There's no shame in doing any job so long as you do it to the best of your ability.' That's the way we were brought up."

By the end of 1951 most of the Estonians had arrived; some, after putting in at least the required six months at Seabrook Farms, had already left to find better-paying jobs and shorter hours in the defense plants and shipyards along the New York-Philadelphia corridor. Pleased by the educational level and work experience of many of the Estonians, the company moved a number of them into supervisory positions. These rapid promotions sometimes angered local residents who had been employed at Seabrook Farms much longer than the Estonians. Albert Vilms wrote about that occasional tension in his diary: "One long-term American worker told me that he had worked in the plant more than ten years and had gotten no advancement, but now men and women come from abroad and are promoted to foremen and foreladies after just a few years. And it did not sit well with some, even outside Seabrook, that these Estonians very soon had new cars and new furniture."

In 1951, C. F., aged seventy and suffering from the aftereffects of what his family believes was a stroke ten years earlier, reluctantly agreed to his son Jack's becoming executive vice president (two years later, C. F. demanded Jack's resignation). Because of C. F.'s health and because the banks whose loans enabled Seabrook Farms to commence each growing season solvent were increasingly concerned about C. F.'s ability to manage the company, the three Seabrook sons were in charge of most day-to-day operations. This fact of life undoubtedly rankled C. F. After all, he was the founder of Seabrook Farms, and he had begun growing the company into one of the largest and most widely mechanized farming operations in America while the "boys" were still in knickers. Perhaps to demonstrate to his sons and to the bankers, and even to himself, that he still had the old zip and could pull off big deals, C. F. decided to fly to Europe the following spring to personally recruit more displaced persons. Jack remains convinced that with the influx of the Japanese Americans and Estonians from 1944 to 1951—a total of some 3,000 men, women, and children—Seabrook Farms didn't need another infusion of labor. He believes his father went to Europe to prove he could do it and to relive as best he could that time thirty years earlier when he sailed the ocean in luxury to run his construction business in Russia and elsewhere. Indeed, one of the reasons the Reverend Herbert Dick had little difficulty in persuading C. F. to sponsor the Estonians is that the Old Man had traveled through the Baltic countries in the 1920s and had been impressed by the people and the scenery.

Many of the families still living in displaced persons camps in Germany when C. F. arrived in 1952 were either homeless German citizens or *volksdeutsch* (ethnic Germans), families who had lived in countries other than Germany for many years, in some cases for centuries, but still held fast to their German heritage and customs. They were a mix of Russians, Ukrainians, Romanians, Yugoslavians, Poles, Czechoslovakians, Bulgarians, and Hungarians. Most of the *volksdeutsch* entered the American and British sectors of Germany in the years after the war as the Soviet Union gradually but relentlessly imprisoned their homelands behind the Iron Curtain. Alan Palmer describes one of the *volksdeutsch* people C. F. brought to America in 1952:

> At the close of the Thirty Years' War in Germany nearly 500 years ago, the ancestors of Alfred Pfannerer left their homeland to move to Silesia and settle in the mountainous area of Czechoslovakia in the region known as Bohemia. Drafted as an eighteen-year-old boy [after Germany occupied Czechoslovakia in 1939], Mr. Pfannerer was sent to Denmark by the German Army. When the war ended, he had no papers which would permit him to work in Germany and was therefore classified as a "stateless person." When he was sponsored by Seabrook Farms, he welcomed the opportunity to come to America. Mr. Pfannerer, who became the coach and manager of the Seabrook Soccer Club, was employed by Seabrook Farms as a mechanic.[9]

Screeners at the displaced persons camps might be forgiven for more than occasionally becoming confused about a person's nationality or national origin. Emma Slavik, who came to work at Seabrook farms, is a case in point. She also grew up in Silesia and considered herself German, but over the centuries that area, which bulges east out of Germany along the Oder River and is prized for its coal mines and steel mills, has changed hands several times. At first a Polish province, it later became a possession of Bohemia (Czechoslovakia); then it became part of Germany (Prussia) in 1742, but was returned to Poland in 1945. To complicate Emma's situation, she reported, she spent time after the war in Bulgaria and married a Yugoslavian. Their daughter, Sabina, was born in a displaced persons camp in Bulgaria.

Another example is Ingrid Hawk, who reported coming to Seabrook with her father and mother when she was four years old. Her parents too were from Silesia when it was part of Germany. Her father had been drafted into the German Army in 1943 and remained in the service until captured by American forces in southeastern Germany toward the end of the war. When he was released from an American prisoner of war camp in Bavaria, he indicated his desire to go back to Silesia. He was told Silesia was now in Poland, which, of course, was under the rule of the Soviet Union, and that he no longer had a home to go back to.

One of the more convoluted explanations of *volksdeutsch* national origin was that provided by another Seabrook worker, Erhardt Wagner. At first, he said he was German; then he said he was born in Poland, or maybe Prussia; no, he corrected himself, actually it was Romania. "I wasn't born in Germany. See, my grandfather wasn't Polish, but when Poland started the uprising against Russia, they wanted the Germans to help in the uprising. So, what they [his grandfather's family] did was move from Poland into the Ukraine. And that's where my father was born, in the Ukraine."

Not all the Germans and *volksdeutsch* who ended up at Seabrook Farms were recruited by C. F. on his trip abroad, although it may be said that those who arrived later came as an indirect result of C. F.'s efforts. A number of Germans and *volksdeutsch* were initially sponsored by individual American farming families in the United States, often through the auspices of the Lutheran Church. Once in this country, having been sponsored by an American family, they heard from relatives or friends who had gone to Seabrook Farms, and the reports made life in New Jersey sound better to them than life where they were living and working at the time.

Edward Falk's parents, from Germany, were guaranteed a home and job by a family who owned a ranch in west Texas, not far from the Mexican border. It was a large spread, he said, several thousand acres of cotton, cattle, and grain. Mr. and Mrs. Falk and their six children—Edward aged eight and three brothers and two sisters ranging in age from five to twelve—arrived in New Orleans aboard an army transport in 1952 and from there traveled to Texas. For a while, the arrangement worked well. In fact, the sponsoring family was so pleased with the work performed by Edward's father that the Falks were offered a small house and ten acres for themselves, and even Mexican farmhands to help. But Mrs. Falk became upset when border patrol agents occasionally came looking for Mexicans who had crossed the border illegally; sometimes there would be shooting. Mrs. Falk had friends who had immigrated to Seabrook Farms, and the letters she received from them indicated that they were very happy being where they were and doing what they were doing. In 1954, the Falks packed their bags and headed east by train to try their luck in New Jersey.

Roman Czelada's father was German and his mother Ukrainian; at the end of the war, he said, his father was "in some kind of prison," and his mother went to work for various farmers in Germany. Roman was five years old. Through the Lutheran Immigration and Relief Service, Mrs. Czelada was also sponsored by a family in Texas, and she and Roman set sail for New Orleans in the fall of 1951. Roman recalled, "The ship had a lot of servicemen on it, and us kids used to get apples, candies, and such from them. I remember seeing my first Mickey Mouse movie on that ship." The ranch was located near Stephenville, about fifty miles southwest of Fort Worth. Living conditions were less than desirable. "When we first moved there they took us to a shack. I remember sleeping in the shack, and at night rats would run across the floor." Sometime after Roman and his mother arrived, his father joined them and was given a job tending cattle and dairy cows. "Once, an armadillo got in the shack and my dad threw a brick at it. That really shook up my mom." Like Mrs. Falk, Mrs. Czelada had friends who had been recruited by C. F. and were pleased with life at Seabrook Farms. In the spring of 1953, just in time for the start of a new growing and harvesting season, the Czelada family boarded a bus and headed for New Jersey by way of Chicago.

The displaced persons, representing a dozen nationalities, substantially added to the global village in numbers and diversity. In the early 1950s it was common to walk into the food processing plant and see, working side by side on the assembly lines in their starched uniforms and caps, women who were African American, Japanese American, Estonian, and *volksdeutsch;* women from the Smoky Mountains of Tennessee and from the foothills of Italy's Apennines. In the fields, shops, garages, and warehouses a visitor could watch Jamaicans pushing green beans through viners, Poles carting boxes of frozen food, and one-time coal miners from West Virginia performing maintenance on Seabrook trucks.

By the mid-1950s, the global village was bursting at the seams and Seabrook Farms was no longer searching the nation and the world for labor. Yet, all was not well in the Seabrook executive offices and bank boardrooms; C. F. and his sons battled for control as loan officers watched nervously. Despite the turmoil within the

Seabrook family and the company, of which most employees had little knowledge, the message being proclaimed to the outside world—and a correct one—was that Seabrook Farms had, indeed, become the "Biggest Vegetable Factory on Earth." That was the title of a feature story in *Life* magazine, which went on to describe the company: "With the mass production adeptness usually associated with motor cars, Seabrook Farms last year [1954] grew, gathered and froze 100 million pounds of 29 vegetables and fruits. Its packaged output of lima beans would have stretched 2,250 miles. Often less than an hour elapses from the time a bean is picked until it is has been washed, sorted, hand-checked, packaged and quick-frozen. Such high-powered activity last year employed 3,200 full- and part-time workers, and grossed a fat $25 million."[10]

At about the same time *Life* was extolling Seabrook Farms, *Quick Frozen Foods,* a trade publication, published a 40-page special section on the company that echoed *Life's* acclaim and further explained why Seabrook Farms then exceeded all other farming operations in America in scope and output: "In addition to growing and processing the crops from its own 19,000 acres, Seabrook Farms absorbs the production of 35,000 acres owned by 1,169 neighboring contract farms. This vast agricultural domain, 54,000 acres of scientifically cultivated soil, spreads across several counties of Southern New Jersey into Delaware, Maryland and Pennsylvania. The Seabrook Farms food-processing plant is the biggest in the world." The company's output in 1955 "was one-tenth of the nation's total pack of frozen fruits and vegetables."[11]

The article continued to point out how Seabrook Farms was the biggest and largest: "The pea and lima bean processing equipment is the plant's major system and the largest assembled anywhere in one spot. Seabrook's french fried potato line is the largest in the East. [The freezing plant] leads the industry." The magazine's editors reported that 1,000 employee families lived in Seabrook Village, and they lauded company policy that ensured that at least one adult in each family would be employed full-time and that other adult members would be promised seasonal work. Courtney Seabrook, who was vice president for marketing at the time, was quoted as predicting that by 1960, Seabrook Farms would grow fruits and vegetables on 100,000 acres and double sales to $50 million.[12] He was wrong in both predictions.

Beyond the Golden Door

Looking back at those times when people from the four corners of America and from both hemispheres of the world worked and lived together, the men and women who were there in the global village as children or young adults marvel at how it all came about—how their parents and grandparents made Seabrook Farms the greatest and the best. In 1995, Liina Keerdoja, whose parents came to Seabrook Farms from Estonia in 1949, tried to put the experience shared by countless hundreds of others in perspective:

> Whenever and wherever I've talked about growing up in Seabrook, people have listened with genuine interest. And why not? Brought into being by force of circumstances and through people the majority of whom would have rather been somewhere else, Seabrook certainly was a novel, if not a unique place. What started out as strange and different had in time become normal and natural. Our ethnic and cultural differences did not disappear, but neither were they a barrier to our getting along. Looking back, I see Seabrook as a playing field of sorts on which we acquired an outlook on life that makes it easier today to live and work and feel at home in a multicultural America. *Multiculturalism,* a popular buzz word of the 1990s, is not a new concept. In Seabrook more than forty years ago, it was already a fact of everyday life.[13]

No matter whether your parents were Dutch, Italian, Estonian, German, Ukrainian, or something else, as a boy growing up in the global village, you soon learned to love American baseball (circa 1945).

The year is 1945. America is at war with Japan, and the parents of these children saluting the American flag have just been released from internment camps.

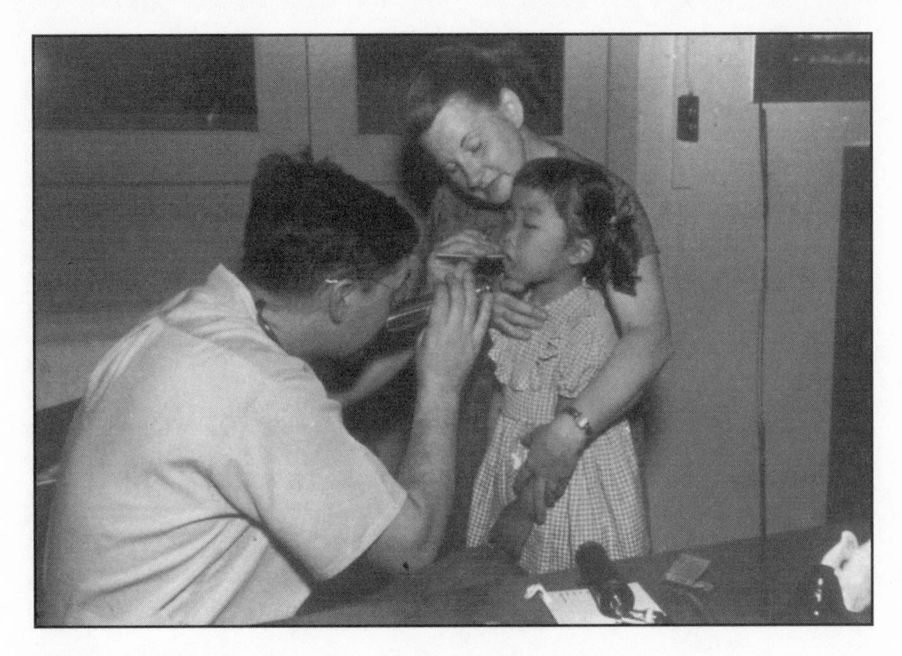

Seabrook Farms had its own infirmary (circa 1945).

The Seabrook Child Care Center was open for children of migrant workers as well as for children of full-time employees (circa 1945).

Ring-around-a-rosy at Seabrook Child Care Center. In the 1940s, Seabrook Farms became one of the first industries to offer on-site child care for workers.

First graders "puttin' on the ritz," (circa 1944).

These boys are preparing their lunch at the day camp sponsored by Seabrook Farms Community House (circa 1950).

Searching for a four-leaf clover at the Child Care Center, 1952.

Many Seabrook workers spoke little or no English when they arrived from internment or displaced persons camps. Seabrook offered English classes at Community House (circa 1952).

Young Japanese Americans (nisei) first helped their parents (issei) prepare to become American citizens; here they assist Europeans in the same way (circa 1952).

The girls' basketball team practicing in the gymnasium at Community House, 1949.

The snack bar at Community House was a favorite hangout for workers both before and after work (circa 1945).

Social life in the global village was centered at Seabrook Community House. Saturday night dances were one of the high spots. Music was supplied by bands composed of employee-musicians or by the jukebox (circa 1945).

John Fuyuume at his piano in Community House (circa 1950).

An Estonian band getting ready to perform, 1952.

Gene Nakata and his Yankee doodlers, 1954.

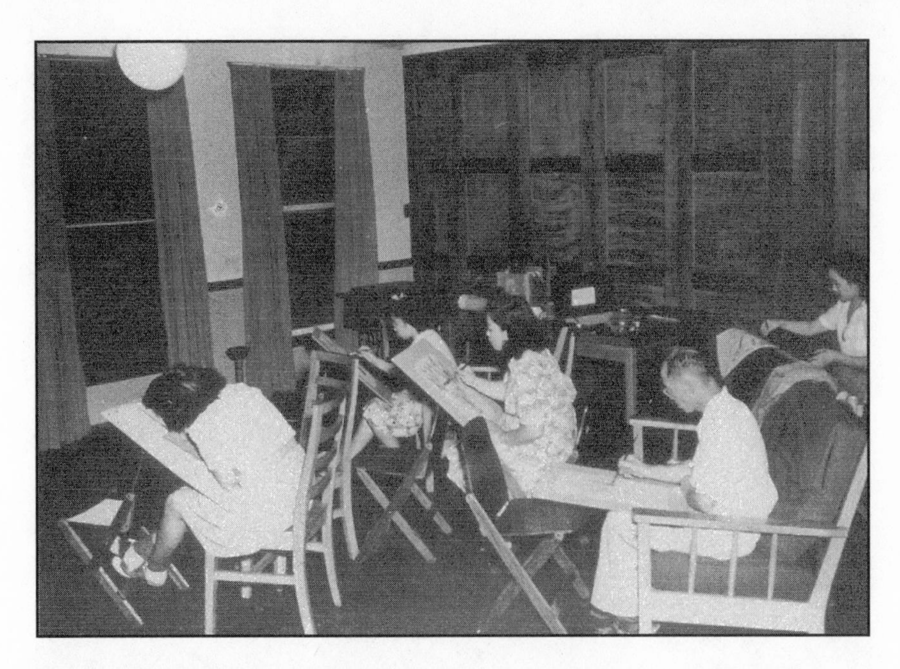

Community House also offered classes in subjects other than English. These men and women are in an art class (circa 1948).

Bridgeton High School students in science class (circa 1950).

Three races and more than twenty-five nationalities or cultures were represented at Seabrook Farms during the first half of the twentieth century (circa 1950).

Three generations of Minyo Dancers, 2002. At left is June Ikeda Mick and at right is her daughter, Stefanie Pierce. The little girl, Danielle Pierce, is Mick's granddaughter. The picture on the wall over Danielle's head shows the original Minyo Dancers at Seabrook Farms in the late 1940s.

The Northville Lutheran Church was built in 1860 by local families named Fox, Hapner, and Garrison. George M. Fox, whose tall monument is in the foreground, was born in 1827. The oldest of the smaller stones marks the grave of Jacob Hapner, who was born thirty-three years before the Declaration of Independence was signed. By the early 1950s, the congregation consisted primarily of Estonian and German immigrants who came to work at Seabrook Farms. The church's graveyard (a portion of which is shown here) now contains dozens of headstones belonging to those immigrants, many of whom died in the last decade of the twentieth century.

Chapter 6

Many Cultures, One Community

In 1947, the second year of the Cold War, Delroy Carey, a field worker from Jamaica, married Allene Meeks. They had met two years before, when she was one of the African American college women flown by Army transport from the Deep South to work in the Seabrook Farms processing plant between the spring and fall semesters. Mr. and Mrs. Carey moved into Hoover Annex, the rude extension of the homely Hoover Village barracks built hurriedly several years earlier to accommodate the rapidly expanding workforce. More than fifty years later, Carey, now a widower living alone in Bridgeton, remembered what life was like in the global village:

> We made friends with Japanese Americans and later with the Estonians, Yugoslavians, Ukrainians—all of them. One of the Estonian or Latvian ladies taught me to polka. We used to have a ball, man. We would sit and talk. [When our daughter was born,] our new friends brought all kinds of gifts for her. Later, in the early 1950s, I had a little car, and I sometimes took people home from the plant. I remember one time I counted eleven heads in the car: Japanese Americans, Estonians—all kinds, all friends. I never charged them anything; they offered gas money, but I said no. They did give us food, vodka, and sake. They were all real nice people; I'll never forget them.

It would be natural, but wrong, to think of Delroy Carey's experience as an exception to the daily life of hundreds of people, many of whom had nothing in common but their desperate need for a job and a place to lie down and rest after working twelve hours. After all, there is every reason to believe that men from the West Indies, African American women, Tennessee hill people and West Virginia coal miners, Japanese Americans, Italian immigrants, and displaced Europeans speaking in foreign tongues, would not associate with one another and would have more than one reason not to like each other. Racial prejudice was still a strong current in America, including South Jersey, in the 1940s and 1950s. We had just fought a terrible war against the Japanese and the Germans, and the media had inundated us with pictures and words showing the brutal nature and bestial visage of our enemies. But the truth is that although enmity and prejudice are always present in some members of every large group, the thoroughly and wonderfully diverse employees of Seabrook Farms made the global village work. Perhaps, as some have said, they had no choice. For many employees—particularly the Japanese Americans forced from their homes and livelihoods on the West Coast and the Europeans bereft of all but prewar memories—Seabrook Farms was a place to start over. For them, life began again at the crossroads of Route 77 and Parsonage Road in Upper Deerfield.

Before taking a closer look at how the people of Seabrook Farms and their cultures commingled, perhaps a consideration of what constituted "the global village" is in order. The global village was really a collection of villages or housing developments, work camps, and individual houses. Most of the permanent living quarters were close enough to the plants and warehouses, and sufficiently dependent on facilities owned by Seabrook Farms or encouraged by it, to be collectively labeled a "company town." For example, many residents initially did most of their shopping at a company store. The so-called Italian Village, which consisted of small houses located near Farm Center, was the first housing development built by Seabrook Farms, and in the beginning it was populated entirely by immigrant Italian families. Later, housing was built behind the Italian Village and was home to families from the West Indies and Tennessee.

When Ellen Nakamura and her two companions came from the Jerome Internment Camp in January 1944 to look over Seabrook Farms, C. F. promised them apartments for families and dormitory rooms for single men and women who agreed to leave the camps and work for the company. He kept his promise—to some degree. The Federal Public Housing Authority (FPHA) had already leased forty-eight acres from Seabrook Farms and was preparing to construct thirty-five buildings containing 200 apartments and eleven dormitories. In addition to housing, the FPHA project included Community House, a large cafeteria, a child care center, a new general store, an infirmary, and administrative offices. Although all this eventually came to pass, the FPHA housing was not sufficient to accommodate all the Japanese Americans who accepted Seabrook's invitation and who arrived sooner and in greater numbers than the company had anticipated and was ready for—2,500 men, women, and children in slightly less than two years. The situation led C. F. to build Hoover Village and Hoover Annex, which became home to the late-arriving Japanese Americans and, later, to transplanted families from the American South and the West Indies and uprooted families from displaced persons camps in Germany. The development was named for a farmer who once owned the property, not for the thirty-first president.

Alan Palmer became housing officer in 1946 and remained in that job for thirty-four years. See Chapter 5 for his description of the prefabricated dwelling units that their residents referred to as barracks (because they resembled barracks and because they were purchased from a lumber company near Fort Dix, one of the major Army bases during and after World War II). Although Palmer, and anyone else who ever lived in or set eyes on Hoover Village and Hoover Annex, pronounced them homely, even ugly, Palmer advised, "Anyone feeling sorry for the families required to live [there] might pause to consider that the units were [rent free and] furnished with beds, tables, chests of drawers and even sheets, blankets, etc. In the early years fuel, in the form of coal briquets, was supplied from a common pile on the edge of each village; even the electricity was unmetered at that time, permitting the workers to save a very substantial portion of their earnings. The accumulation of savings had a high priority in the ambitions of the people who had come to Seabrook with no assets other than their ability to work." Plant workers in the middle and late 1940s earned between fifty-seven and sixty-nine cents an hour and, when production was in high gear twenty-four hours a day seven days a week, they might work seventy-two hours a week. If both husband and wife worked in the plants, (on different shifts) which was customary, a family that came to Seabrook with only a few dollars and change in their pockets could, if they were fortunate, bring in between $82 and $100 each week. Seabrook office workers, on the other hand, earned a flat $25 for a six-day week, eight hours a day. Moreover, especially in the days before the company installed electric ranges and refrigerators, most residents of Hoover Village and Hoover Annex ate in the company cafeteria, located in Community House, and were charged an amount "below the actual cost of the food."[1]

Three other housing developments for permanent workers were designated School Village, West Village, and Gunnison Village. All three were in close proximity to the plants. Visualize Route 77 running north and south and Parsonage Road running east and west. The processing plants, cold storage warehouse, and major shops were located on Parsonage Road west of its intersection with Route 77, and the intersection was roughly at the center of the major housing developments (exclusive of Italian Village). The FPHA project, including Community House, extended from the southeast corner of the intersection, with Hoover Village and Hoover Annex behind and south of it. School Village, which consisted of twenty-two older houses, was at the northeast corner near the school, naturally. West Village and Gunnison Village were located back from the northwest corner.

West Village, which was constructed at about the same time as the displaced persons from Europe began to arrive, consisted of eighty bungalows with basements. Unlike the housing of the FPHA project, Hoover Village and Hoover Annex, these bungalows were reserved primarily for supervisory personnel. Moreover, a person's position and sometimes his or her relationship with company executives (including but not necessarily limited to C. F.), helped determine whether that person moved into West Village. "At that time it was not a matter of an employee stating he wished to rent one of the new bungalows in West Village. His application was reviewed by a committee, which determined whether or not he qualified for the assignment and whether or not someone still higher in the company echelon desired him to be given consideration. In the desperate post-war shortage of housing, anyone who got one of the bungalows felt he had passed a real test of worth." The company charged $35 a month rent, not bad for a department head who might be earning $350 a month "on the top secret monthly payroll prepared and seen only by the Treasurer of Seabrook Farms. . . ." West Village bungalows were accessed from Route 77 via First and Second Streets.[2]

Work began on Gunnison Village shortly after the bungalows in West Village were ready for occupancy. Gunnison Village, which also consisted of eighty houses, was a step down from West Village. The prefabricated plywood houses were assembled in Pennsylvania by a subsidiary of U.S. Steel and placed on concrete slabs. These houses were arranged in rows just north of West Village on Third and Fourth Streets. Their opening in 1952 concluded the major construction of housing at Seabrook Farms. However, the Housing Office was also responsible for maintaining and assigning approximately 150 farmhouses situated in the vicinity of Seabrook Farms and northwest into Salem County, which had been acquired as the tracts of farmland were purchased. When all the housing units included in the global village were in place, Alan Palmer was "the titular landlord to well over [1,000] heads of family [permanent employees] who had signed the month-to-month leases."[3] Most temporary or seasonal workers lived in a dozen or so camps maintained on the same number of farming divisions scattered over South Jersey and into southeastern Pennsylvania, Delaware, and a slice of Maryland. In most cases, seasonal and migrant farmworkers lived in barracks, or what the company called "hutments," prefabricated structures that measured sixteen by sixteen feet. The camps had central toilet and shower facilities, and meals were served in the camps. Life in the camps was primitive. Many of the regulations designed to improve the lot of migrant workers had not yet been enacted by New Jersey and other states in the 1940s and 1950s.

Life in the global village revolved around the workplace, and for many men and women it meant performing tasks for which they had no training and, often, to which they had a strong aversion. Recall Albert Vilms, the lawyer and mayor from Estonia, who spent his first night at the end of a fast-moving assembly line—an alien in an alien environment in an alien land. James Mitsui, married and father of two little girls, had worked on his father's small fruit orchard in California before World War II and internment at the Jerome camp in Arkansas. When he arrived at Seabrook Farms in the late spring of 1944, he was assigned to the cold storage operation and immediately joined a diverse crew. His supervisor was Don Ittolieto, son of an Italian immigrant, and his coworkers included a young man whose parents were Native Americans and lived on a reservation, an African American college student from Mississippi, and two German prisoners of war. Mitsui remembered: The POWs were "young people like our own Americans, you know, and we got to know them pretty well. They were human beings [like us] and we worked together. Gosh, I came [to Seabrook Farms] as a displaced person myself—and I'm an American. They were impressed with the way we treated them. When it was time for them to leave, one of the men said to me, 'Jim, when I go back to Germany, I want to come back to America.'"

Over the next few years many of the Italian supervisors who had worked at Seabrook Farms since the 1930s retired and were replaced by Japanese Americans. Later still, some of the Japanese American supervisors in the plant were replaced by Estonians, although many of the Estonian men, because of their college education and previous experience, moved up through the ranks in various administrative offices rather than assuming supervisory roles in the plant.

Emma Slavik, one of the *volksdeutsch,* worked on the packing line. "Oh, those hours! We packed spinach, lima beans, and French beans. The French beans took the longest time, and you had to finish the work. Sometimes we worked twelve hours a day, seven days a week, without a day off. If [before the shift began] it was raining, we were so glad. We said, 'Oh, gosh, maybe they won't call us because there won't be any work.'" Unfortunately, on rainy days in Seabrook it was not raining in the faraway fields where the beans were coming from. The boss of the packing line was a Japanese American man; the foreladies were from Latvia, Estonia, and Tennessee. "The woman from Tennessee was nasty at first; I don't think she liked us [Europeans], but later on we got along pretty good." Others on the line included women from Russia, Romania, Yugoslavia, and Hungary. "One of my best friends was Hungarian, and we're still friends," Slavik said. "We worked together [then], and now we live together in the same building; she's on the floor above me."

John Melchiorre, who started working for the Dutch nurserymen after graduation from Bridgeton High School in 1940, remembers when the company first brought African Americans into the plant. Before World War II, African American men and women worked exclusively in the fields. "These were local black women, mostly from Bridgeton. I can still visualize that first group in their uniforms [blue with white cap] marching off to peel potatoes. We thought at first there might be friction with [white women], but there wasn't." Soon thereafter, two African American men were hired to work in the plant. "That was the beginning [of placing African Americans] in the plant." After the war, Melchiorre served in a number of top administrative positions, and he witnessed the rapid and amazing growth of the global village. "It was amazing because everybody had a job to do, and they all knew that it was hard work. But no one seemed to complain. We never had a problem with all the different cultures. They all seemed to get along."

The workplace included children, especially in the summer months. "I started digging bulbs when I was eight years old," remembered Robert Busnardo, grandson of an Italian immigrant and former resident of the Italian Village. "I was fired because I wasn't strong enough to pick up the bushel basket. You didn't get paid unless you could bring the basket [full of daffodil or gladiola bulbs] to the end of the row; I couldn't even drag the basket. [Mr. Gerard Overdevest, the Dutchman who supervised the garden] said, 'You're a good worker, Bobby, but I can't have you doing this, because the other boys are helping you [with the baskets], and that's taking away from their work. We can't have that." When he was a year or two older, Busnardo frequently took part in what can only be described as a shape-up. A group of boys—Italians mostly but also children of Tennessee families who lived behind Italian Village—gathered under the water tower and waited to get hired for the day. Usually, their employer du jour was Overdevest. "If he needed ten kids and there were fifteen under the tower, only ten worked. After he got to know me, I was one of his top hands, and he'd say, 'Bobby, get in the front seat with me and let the rest ride in the back [of the truck.]' We were all young—nine, ten, and eleven—but that's when we went into the fields. And of course Seabrook controlled all of this. I mean every inch was Seabrook, and everything that you did was Seabrook; every piece of land was Seabrook."

A good portion of Seabrook land was devoted to the growing of lima beans and green beans, and most boys wound up in the bean fields by age twelve, some sooner. "We tried to get in the bean field before we were allowed to," said Estonian Reverend Toomas Vaga. "I always say proudly that I bought my first bicycle with my earnings from my first year in the bean field, which was forty-five dollars. And I had ten dollars left over."

Paul Noguchi remembered how thrilled he was when he got his summer working papers and joined "the ranks of my playmates to work in the bean fields which surrounded the Seabrook area." He had to get up very early in the morning to catch a bus that left for the fields from Community House. "Most of my Japanese American friends and classmates were present, as were Estonians, Germans and Latvians. I remember the anticipation of whether the sun would be hot or whether it would be cloudy; [it was very] uncomfortable after a rainfall because the plants were all wet and our clothes became soaked." The boys were assigned cards that were punched as they brought in baskets of beans to be weighed; each full basket weighed about twenty-three pounds. Occasionally, a boy would pour a little water from the water truck in his basket to up the weight, and occasionally a checker would catch him at it. "I remember the good-natured Puerto Rican and Jamaican workers who were always willing to add their 'overs' if we came up a bit short at weighing time." The humdrum of the long, sizzling days was frequently interrupted by Jamaicans singing and sometimes by Jamaicans chasing rabbits that ran through the fields.[4]

One of the features of Seabrook Farms the *Reader's Digest* article of January 1944 cited for special mention was the Child Care Center, probably because in the 1940s child care outside the family was not widespread anywhere in society, let alone among the nation's industries. The center operated from morning to late afternoon. In many cases both parents worked for the company on different shifts. The parent who worked the night shift could sleep during the day, and the other parent dropped off their children at the Child Care Center and went to work on the day shift. If the workplace was a melting pot of prodigious dimensions, the center served as a complementary diminutive mixing bowl. Peeter Vilms remembers being there at age five in the summer of 1949. "I had never been separated from family, but there were others in the same straits. That helped, [even though] many of them spoke no Estonian whatsoever. I remember large circles of kids sitting cross-legged on the floor echoing in unison the teacher: 'Say fork!' as she held up a fork, and 'Say knife!' when it was the knife's turn."[5]

Most of the parents worked ten- or twelve-hour shifts from spring to fall, and their dedication to task and to finally getting back on their feet after years of being uprooted, transplanted, and displaced, although exemplary, took its toll. "Though I was young, I was constantly aware of the hardships our parents endured," said Reet Sikkemae. "[They spent] long, miserable, hot hours at the factory and [got] little sleep. I was silently relieved whenever my mother got home early, so she could get rest, not realizing the financial hardship this would cause because of the short days. Many people lost their health from this strenuous work and usually spent the winter recuperating in and out of doctors' offices and hospitals."[6]

Although the residents of the global village often worked shoulder to shoulder with men or women of a different color and from a foreign land, and although a coworker who was a stranger at first might become a good friend, people were more apt to become close friends off the job. The intermingling most often occurred at Community House, but sometimes in their living quarters, at picnics and other events sponsored by the company, and even at local watering holes like the Chicken Coop, the Garden Inn, and the Landis Tavern. Cultures were both shared and preserved. Latvians and Estonians, for example, might be willing—even eager—to show a Jamaican how to polka, but they also wanted to preserve their language, customs, and costumes for their children and their children's children.

Community House, which the USO (United Service Organizations) operated during World War II, was the social hub of the village. It offered something for nearly everyone: cafeteria, snack bar, lounge, small gymnasium that also served as auditorium, theater (movies on Tuesdays and Thursdays for ten cents), and dance floor (featuring a juke box and sometimes bands composed of Seabrook workers), pool and billiards room, and club rooms used by ethnic groups, Boy Scout and Girl Scout troops, and classes where one could learn a craft or a foreign language (English for many people). In addition to all of those functions, church services, weddings, and funerals were often conducted at Community House. Reet Sikkemae remembers as a child going to Community House to see movies and watch Howdy Doody and Willie the Worm on television. "I also got some books from the library and played a little Ping-Pong and volleyball."[7] For Ann Mariko Lowe, Friday was basketball night in the gym. She and other Japanese American girls organized two teams, the Pandas and the Bobby-soxers. The gym was small by today's standards. "We didn't get to run back and forth the entire court like the girls do today. Our forwards played on one half the court and the guards on the other half. We were allowed only three dribbles and then had to pass the basketball to another player."[8]

Talent shows in the Community House auditorium always drew crowds, and often the shows imitated or poked fun at radio, and later, television programs and performers popular at the time. Sam Seno, a Japanese American who worked in the welding shop, acted as master of ceremonies. On the night of August 11, 1945, he introduced "Radio Reveries": "This is Station USO broadcasting from our studio in Seabrook Hotel." Both the cast and audience came in three colors. For example, in a spoof of daytime soap operas, William Wakatsuki played Rodney in "Rodney Hossenfeffer's Other Wife," and Bethel Alexander, an African American, played the other wife. In a take-off of the *Major Bowes Amateur Hour,* which had once given a very young Frank Sinatra his first national audience, Samah Pearson, Jamaican, played a guitar solo, Tak Yamamoto sang "The More I See You," and Betty Hakes, from the local Caucasian community, sang, "The Hills of Home." The company newspaper later that month reported: "The high quality of the talent and clever lines drew enthusiastic applause from a capacity audience which called for encore after encore."[9] On other nights, the Minyo dancers, robed in brilliantly colored kimonos, might perform, and after the Estonians arrived, their costumed choir or folk dancers might take the stage.

Emiko Noguchi Herold, a teenager at the time, recalled that a bookmobile parked outside Community House every fourteen days. "I used to go inside this mobile library each time it came around and spend perhaps a half hour browsing through books. How difficult it was to choose the three [books] that each person was allowed to take out! Somehow the kind man who drove the movable library must have noticed my problem, and he allowed me to borrow an added book or two. Through those books I traveled the world [and learned] about interesting people."[10]

Community House sponsored a number of outings during the warm weather. These provided workers and their families with much-needed breaks from the grinding tedium experienced in the fields and plants that were turning out frozen and dehydrated food twenty-four hours a day. The events included picnicking, fishing, swimming, boating, and softball games at nearby Parvin State Park. During the war, the USO also transported groups to the seashore "within travel limits established by the OPA [Office of Price Administration, which rationed gasoline and other products]." Outdoor sports were popular with all age groups, except that most of the Europeans didn't catch on to baseball for a while and the Jamaicans preferred to play cricket.

Community House served its highest calling in 1948 when it became the site of a citizenship class for Japanese men and women (issei) who had immigrated to the United States long before World War II but had been denied citizenship by the current immigration law. For nearly five years, the local chapter of the Japanese American Citizens League (JACL) and American Legion Post 95 in Bridgeton sponsored such classes under the direction of Mrs. Herbert Brauer. The Post 95 is believed to have been the first American Legion unit in the country to involve itself in such a program. Referring to this period, Michi Nishiura Weglyn, who had spent time at Seabrook Farms, wrote, "The status of being perpetual aliens came to an end for the issei when the right to become American citizens was granted them in their twilight years with the passage of the Walter-McCarran Immigration and Naturalization Act of 1952. The 'ineligibility for citizenship' clause was made forever void; it nullified, in turn, hundreds of discriminatory laws and ordinances throughout the country historically designed to keep people of Asian origin 'in their place.'"[11] Both the JACL and the post proudly point out that the Seabrook classes began *before* passage of the Walter-McCarran Immigration and Naturalization Act.

On June 29, 1953, 126 issei were finally granted their citizenship by Judge David Horowitz in a ceremony at the Seabrook School. Up to that point, it was the largest group of individuals of a single nationality ever to be naturalized at the same time in the United States. Among the new citizens were Mrs. Minakata, Mrs. Fujiki, and Mrs. Mukai, all Gold Star mothers. Their sons had enlisted in the 442nd Regimental Combat Team, composed entirely of all Japanese Americans, and had given their lives for their country in Europe, while their own government kept their parents behind barbed wire. In a move typifying the goodwill that people of the global village often extended to each other, children of these new citizens (nisei) later helped the Europeans register for United States citizenship.

The term *multiculturalism* did not enter the American lexicon until late in the twentieth century, but in the middle of the century multiculturalism was first outside the front doors of homes in the global village. "When I was growing up in Seabrook, I used to marvel, because you would go outside and there would be kids talking in Japanese to a kid who was talking in German and another one who was [speaking] Spanish, and they all seemed to understand what they were saying," said Fusaye Kazaoka. She was fourteen when her family came to Seabrook. She remembers Mongolians living down the street, speaking still another language, probably Chinese or Russian. "They were all Buddhist, too, but they were a different sect. [They] all wore bright saffron robes [to worship services,] and they prostrated themselves in front of the altar."[12] Eventually, the Japanese Americans who were Buddhists built their own temple on Northville Road, and a number of the Christian Japanese Americans attended the Deerfield Presbyterian Church, which also was well attended and heavily supported by the Seabrook family. In time, most of the Europeans who were Lutheran attended Estonian- and German-language services at the old Lutheran Church on Burlington Road, a half-hour walk from Hoover Village, where today tombstones bearing such Estonian names as Tammaru and Poldma far outnumber those on the graves of the Fox family, who were among the church's founders in 1859. When they first arrived, however, people of nearly all faiths conducted worship services at Community House.

"Assimilation [where we lived in the village] just came naturally," recalls Edward Falk, whose parents were German. "No one said you had to get along with this group or that group. No one made a big deal about what you were. There was no active segregation of any ethnic group. I think that children were much more liberal in their views than the parents. Our parents knew who was Polish and who was Ukrainian and who was Estonian, but the children didn't really care. We were all in the same boat."

Rei Noguchi glimpsed life in the housing developments as a kid delivering the *Bridgeton Evening News* on his bike:

> I remember walking home [from school,] unloading my books on my bed and grabbing my ink-stained canvas delivery bag off the doorknob of my room. I [hopped] on my maroon [and] plain vanilla, mail-order, 26-inch middleweight bicycle [and rode] east down Second Street, crossing Route 77 to the older part of the village to . . . the newspaper depot of Seabrook. [I started my route

by] turning left on Parsonage Road and pedaling toward the General Store, past the other side of Community House, past the remodeled dormitory facing Seabrook Village [the federal housing project,] and past Mr. Fujimoto's TV repair shop. I remember coasting in and out of Van Buren, Roosevelt, Flower and Juniper Streets [and seeing] at the ends of these streets little vegetable gardens the residents had planted. I [rode] through the dirt passageways of Hoover Annex and experienced a sense of apprehension and mystery since I recognized no one of my own age in this area.

I remember weaving between the tightly packed rows of rectangular buildings, where rows and buildings seemed almost indistinguishable from the next, where gray skies seemed to blend in with the gray buildings and their black-tarred roofs. I remember sometimes seeing residents (Germans, Japanese, Polish and other displaced peoples of World War II), mostly adults, emerging from the buildings and heading to the communal washrooms and showers or returning home with bags of groceries from the General Store. I remember wondering what it would be like to live in Hoover Annex day after day, what unexplored secrets its somber living units held, what its residents were really like, what stories they could tell of their former and distant homelands. I remember seeing to the south of the Annex buildings, across a stretch of vegetable gardens, the stark outlines of Hoover Village, a place perhaps just as mysterious to me as Hoover Annex, but here my paper route did not extend, but secretly I wished it did. I wonder now, just as I did then, who could speak for these residents of Hoover Village and Hoover Annex to make known their past and daily lives.[13]

Ida Mueller Hintz is one of many Seabrook residents who have told their stories. She grew up in the Ukraine, but fled to

Germany with her mother at the start of World War II after the Russians rounded up educated men and large landowners, which included her father, and dispatched them to Siberia. She and her mother arrived at Seabrook in the early 1950s, along with other *volksdeutsche,* and there she found another family. "If there was an event [at someone's apartment or at Community House], everybody was invited. It was not just the Germans or just the Polish or just the Japanese. Even now . . . they're all like family. They're all hugging [and saying] 'nice to see you.'" Ida met her future husband at a community dance, and they were married four years later. "We had a big wedding. I had no relatives here except my immediate family, but as a stranger coming here, everybody was our family, so everybody was invited. There were Germans, Polish, Russians, Japanese—whoever I worked with. We made our own food. My friends cooked the food, they baked, and they served. Even today they talk about it."[14]

Sometimes two stories intersect at a particular time and place in the past, even when both parties are widely separated at the moment they remember. That was the case with Jack Seabrook and Samah Pearson. Speaking on the telephone from his office in Mannington, New Jersey, in the late fall of 2001, Seabrook recalled the day in 1943 when a large group of men he had recruited in the Jamaican countryside arrived by train at Husted Station, then located several miles from Farm Center. The men stood silently in long rows on the station platform. "I stood in front of them not knowing exactly what to say or do." He decided to break the embarrassing silence by asking for any man who knew how to drive a truck to step forward. Every one of them moved ahead. Years later, in the displaced persons camps in Germany, when screeners who were looking for farm workers asked men and women desiring to emigrate to America whether they had farming experience, nearly everyone answered affirmatively, no matter what job they had held before the war. "Yes" could mean a ticket across the Atlantic; "no" almost assuredly meant spending another week, another month, another year in the holding camp where they had been biding their time for as long as five or six years. That fall afternoon in 2001, Seabrook remembered Samah Pearson taking an extra step forward and volunteering to organize the men according to their skills. Seabrook was both amazed and relieved.

It was the beginning of a warm relationship both in and out of the workplace.

In 1994, six years before his death, Pearson was interviewed for a collection of oral histories recorded for the Seabrook Educational and Cultural Center. The interviewer, who apparently knew something of that event in 1943, asked Pearson to tell what had happened. "Well, some of the particulars I don't remember. I do recall that when we came out in groups, I did say something to [Mr. Seabrook], 'Let's do this,' you know. I'm being honest with you; I don't remember any more than that." (He was also being very modest). Eventually, Pearson was given almost full responsibility for the workers recruited from the West Indies. When he finally retired from Seabrook Farms, Jack Seabrook arranged with New Jersey Civil Service to have him employed as an inspector of migrant labor camps. "My impression of [Jack] Seabrook then and now is that he was one of the kindest persons you could ever meet. The way he treated people, you wouldn't think he was the big Mr. Seabrook. He treated you like a person, a real person. He was a wonderful person, and I'll never forget him."[15]

At Seabrook Farms in the 1940s and 1950s, the many cultures and customs that existed then in the global village seldom clashed, but they frequently challenged, surprised, and delighted the residents. "I remember our first experience with Trick or Treat," said Ann Mariko Lowe, "when a white boy came knocking at our door and my mother [who was a Japanese alien at the time] not knowing what to do. A few years later, everyone knew about Halloween."[16] Another Japanese woman, Harumi Taniguchi, who had just arrived at Seabrook, encountered an African American person for the first time while standing in line at the cafeteria in Community House. A very tall black man came up behind the tiny Mrs. Taniguchi and said with a broad smile, "Welcome to New Jersey, mama!" Mrs. Taniguchi said it was the nicest thing anyone had said to her since her arrival from the interment camp.[17] Ingrid Hawk, who, with her parents, walked off the troop ship *John Muir* in New York in 1952 at age four, had never seen an African American person before coming to Seabrook Farms from Germany. But it didn't matter. In an interview she said, "So, there's a person that's black, or there's a person who has eyes different than me. It didn't dawn on me until I was an adult that [life at

Seabrook Farms] was something unique. I got out of high school in 1965, and that was when all the civil rights activism was going on. That's when I became aware that there were other areas in the country that didn't behave like we did. I mean, I heard about segregated bathrooms and other things and thought, What are you talking about? I never heard of such a thing." Most of the immigrants from Europe had never seen Asians. Helgi Malleus Viire remembers being fascinated by Japanese American men and women. "I had never seen other ethnic peoples [in Estonia], and I was fascinated when older Japanese men and women [issei] would greet you by bowing. And I thought they were so beautiful. Their hair was almost blue-black shiny. I was a very shy child then, and I would just be quiet and just watch everyone. I enjoyed—really enjoyed—all the differences."

If a new arrival knew only Estonian or German or Lithuanian or another of the many languages spoken at Seabrook Farms, that person likely would encounter difficult and sometimes embarrassing situations until he or she learned enough English to get by. Maimu Miido, who directed the Estonian Mixed Chorus at Seabrook, recalled the time when a woman whose native language was German decided she needed a pillow to sit on at work because her metal seat at the assembly line always felt cold. She asked a co-worker where she could buy a pillow, and she was directed to a store in Bridgeton. When she visited the store and the clerk asked her what she wanted, she replied, "I vant a *kissen* [the German word for pillow.]" Surprised, the clerk asked, "You want a kiss on your cheek?" "No, I want it here," she replied, patting her rear end.

Seabrook Farms sponsored English language classes at Community House, but many people acquired the language from fellow workers, television shows—even comic books. Ida Mueller Hintz learned English from a variety of sources. "We watched a lot of movies, you know, the drive-in movies. They were pretty cheap and that's how we learned. And from people. The nice thing about it was [that] you could talk backwards, crooked, any way, and no one would make fun of you. Everybody would help you. I think that was wonderful. Later, I learned through my children. They went to school, and I went to school with them, because they came home with homework, and I had to work with them."[18]

Josie Ikeda volunteered to teach English to European immigrants. "Three or four of us [Japanese Americans] taught classes. Of course, it was in the winter, because in the summer they all had to work very long [hours.]" A Harvard professor who had pioneered a system for teaching languages through word–picture association met with the Japanese American teachers in New York before they commenced teaching their classes at Seabrook. "It was surprising how fast the young people learned just by association, pictures, and things like that; they learned very fast," said Josie. Sometimes, the classes would take field trips to New York, Washington, or Valley Forge. "I remember this woman [on a trip to Washington] saying, 'Oh my goodness, the president lives in a small house.' Whoever ruled her country [must have] lived in a big palace, so she thought that [the President living in the White House] was funny. Another thing she commented on was the lack of statuary [in Washington]. I guess where she came from, every corner had a statue of somebody or something."[19]

If Seabrookers of different races and cultures clashed, it was generally outside the global village, and alcohol was the principal instigator. Upper Deerfield, where Seabrook Farms is situated, was and still is a dry township. Not so neighboring Deerfield Township, and the main hangouts were the Chicken Coop, the Garden or Hamilton Inn (the name varies according to people's memory), and the Landis Tavern. The Chicken Coop was a chicken coop converted into a rustic (some might say dilapidated) bar. It was frequented primarily by Tennessee employees. "There was always a fight there Friday and Saturday nights," Ernest "Dooley" Holt remembers. "Nobody got hurt bad, and the next day they were friends." The drinkers at the Garden/Hamilton Inn were a more diverse lot: white southerners, seasonal Puerto Ricans, local people both white and black, and some Europeans. "If you really wanted a fight, you would go there," said Holt. "But again, it was a fist fight and that was all, and the next day it would be all right." Juhan Simonson remembers how "it didn't really matter" who you were or where you came from when you sat on a barstool. "I mean, if you mentioned that you were from Estonia, most people thought that was someplace in Pennsylvania. So, we never went into explanations."

One of the best parts of culture sharing was discovering new food or different ways to prepare food. The Reverend Toomas Vaga arrived at Seabrook from a displaced persons camp in Germany in the spring of 1949. "I will never forget . . . the first time I experienced the mysterious food called spaghetti in the school lunchroom," he said. Sabina Slavik Woodward, who was born in a displaced persons camp, still recalls with relish enjoying her first ice cream cone under the Seabrook Farms tower. A camp for Jamaicans was located behind the Italian Village, and the cookhouse that served the camp offered both a challenge and an education, according to Robert Busnardo, who was one of the Italian boys who came to know, like, and sometimes bedevil the Jamaican who once told them, "I am the cookie, mon." Of course, thereafter, he was "the cookie man" to the boys. "The cookie man would sometimes feed us. That's where I learned how to eat rice and mutton. They were mutton people, and we had never had mutton." Radio was big in the 1940s, and for young boys the biggest thing on the radio was the late afternoon serial Captain Midnight. A young listener could get a Captain Midnight decoder ring by sending in labels from containers of Ovaltine, the program's sponsor. "None of us could afford Ovaltine, but one day when we went to the cookhouse, lo and behold, cookie man had stacks—cases—of Ovaltine. A couple of kids would fool around and distract cookie man, and the rest of us would take labels." Cookie man finally caught on to what the boys were doing and scolded them. "'Don't take the labels,'" he would say, but we outsmarted him, every time."

Many centuries before the Italians, Jamaicans, Japanese Americans, Estonians, and all the others came to people the global village, the land that constituted Seabrook Farms was lived on and cultivated by the Lenni Lenape tribe, which belonged to the Delaware family of Native Americans. In 1832, Wilted Grass, a Lenni Lenape then living in Wisconsin, returned to negotiate the sale of his tribe's remaining land rights to the state. He concluded his business by issuing this statement: "Not a drop of our blood have you spilled in battle; not an acre of our land have you taken but by our consent. These facts speak for themselves and need no comment."[20] Now, at last, the diverse community of men, women, and children who lived and worked and played on a corner of that ancient land from 1900 to 1960 has spoken for itself in these pages.

Chapter 7

Reading, 'Riting, and Respect

In 1947, New Jersey passed a law prohibiting racial segregation in its public schools, thus becoming the first state in the nation to do so. Of course, the Charles F. Seabrook School had been desegregated since its opening twenty-two years earlier, and in the late 1940s its classrooms contained not only children of African American and West Indian employees of Seabrook Farms, but also Japanese American and Estonian children. By the mid-1950s, the school would enroll boys and girls whose roots tapped twenty-five nationalities or cultures. The Seabrook School in the first half of the twentieth century was unlike almost any other school in rural America.

The Seabrook School, in 1923, was one of the first consolidated schools—kindergarten through grade eight—to serve predominantly farming families. Its children lived either in the Seabrook Farms company town or on farms in bucolic Upper Deerfield Township that were under contract to Seabrook Farms. When it opened, the school immediately replaced four small schoolhouses at Farm Center, each of which had contained two grades. It was the first school in the area to boast indoor plumbing.

For most American children, the first day of school in August or September arrives at just the right time. Whether they will admit it or not, the lazy summer days that stretched out so invitingly back in May or June have dragged into boredom, and the children look forward to seeing friends they haven't seen since everyone ran for the school exits on the last day. For two children who had grown up in Upper Deerfield, opening day in September 1944 was unlike any other they—or anyone else, for that matter—had ever experienced.

"I remember the excitement I felt when I went to school that year," recalled Elaine Glendon Laws. "I had attended Seabrook School since I was five years old, arriving each morning on the school bus that picked me up in front of my house on the Vineland Pike. Suddenly, everything had changed. There were two fifth grades. Not only that, but the classrooms were half filled with strangers! Unheard of in this small farming community where we had all known each other our whole lives, traipsing across the fields to play in each other's houses."[1] The strangers were the Japanese American children of families who had arrived at Seabrook Farms in large numbers over the summer. Alan Woodruff, whose family grew peas and bush lima beans for Seabrook Farms, remembered the same day, when he started the fourth grade: "It was a terribly exciting time in the school when the student population increased almost fifty percent overnight. The whole atmosphere changed."[2]

Elaine found the Japanese American girls "absolutely fascinating." She elaborated, "They had black, shiny hair and the whitest teeth. Comparing their features to my unruly blond pigtails and freckled face, I thought they were downright beautiful. And they were so sophisticated! Now, of course, I realize they must have been a bit wary of us . . . at that age I was too insensitive to realize their lives were not idyllic."[3] Having just come from internment camps where white America had confined them and their parents behind barbed wire for two years, they had every reason to be fearful of the reception that awaited them in southern New Jersey, where the only Japanese most people had ever seen were in propaganda films that depicted them as yellow, buck-toothed brutes. Even the management of Seabrook Farms, which had recruited the Japanese Americans, saw nothing wrong or inconsistent when page one of the June 1945 issue of *The Seabrooker* featured a headline over the lead article that read "Smalley Serving on LST That Beat Off Japs at Iwo" and, at the bottom of the same page, displayed a two-column by five-inch photo showing "friendly, efficient Dick Kunishima," who managed the company store and the cafeteria.

Robert Busnardo, who lived in the Italian Village, admits to being a "rough, nasty little thing" when he was a kid in Seabrook School in the 1940s. "When the Japanese came, they really improved our lot in life in a lot of ways. Of course, I'm not gonna lie to you, we hated their guts. [In 1944–45] they were the enemy. My father told me that when the Japanese were first hired, [the other employees] were all told that anyone that messed with the Japanese would lose their job. They were to be treated kindly, without any malice and stuff like that. That was easy to say. I had three uncles that I loved dearly. They were all in the war, one in the Pacific and two in Germany. [The uncle in the Pacific] was in the invasion of Tarawa, so he'd seen some [bad things]. And I'll never forget the look on his face when he came home on leave." Busnardo egged on the Japanese American students every chance he got. "They would fight back. They were American kids, so they had gangs, too—the Yellow Jackets. They proved themselves. They were meaner than hell. At first, there were a lot of fights. Then it quieted down and they were somewhat accepted."

Busnardo's open hostility toward Japanese American kids of his own age was very much the exception rather than the rule. Although Seabrook Farms management and school and community leaders often worried about local reaction to the rapid influx of Japanese Americans during the latter years of World War II, the response was never as bad as they feared it could be. Seabrook teenagers attended grades nine through twelve at Bridgeton High

School, and Jack Seabrook remembers the first night a Bridgeton basketball team that included Japanese Americans was scheduled to take to the floor in a league game. "I got a call from the [Bridgeton] mayor, who was upset because the local newspaper had just published a picture showing the Japanese beheading one of the American pilots who had been captured from the Doolittle raid [more than two years earlier]. He wondered if we should call off the game. I thought we should do nothing in advance, but suggested we attend the game and be prepared to take action on the spot if things got out of hand." The game was played without incident.

A Japanese American high school student wrote an essay in which she recounted how, in the fall of 1944, she and other Japanese American students feared rejection but instead encountered acceptance.

> We left [the internment] camp with a quaking heart. How would the people accept us? Would there be prejudice? It was with such a feeling that we nisei entered our first "real" high school in Bridgeton. . . . A great many of us being in camp for two years or more had not attended any high school other than the one in camp. To our relief and happiness, Bridgeton High School welcomed us with warm hearts. Probably the students and teachers do not know actually how much their friendliness has meant to all the Japanese students. Never before had we been given such an uplift of feeling. Our general reaction was, "Say, this is all right! We're right in with the rest of them." We, who felt unwanted and cast off, began to feel like someone again. Without realizing it, the people [teachers, administrators, and others] through their kindness helped countless citizens regain their faith in the United States.[4]

Alice Kinoshita, author of the essay, was wrong about only one thing. Teachers and administrators at Seabrook School and

Bridgeton High School *did* realize and then willingly accepted the challenge of helping not only the Japanese Americans, but children who had experienced the horrors of war in Europe and didn't speak English, African American children who still confronted prejudice not far from the schoolyard, and children whose parents had been uprooted and transplanted from pockets of poverty and hopelessness in Appalachia. Henry Ward Beecher, distinguished orator in the last half of the nineteenth century and brother to Harriet Beecher Stowe, once proclaimed in a sermon that people "are products, expressions, reflections; they live to the extent that they coincide with their epoch, or to the extent that they differ markedly from it."[5] Fortunately, for the multifarious classes that swelled both schools in the 1940s and 1950s, and for the larger society they entered upon graduation, their teachers and administrators almost perfectly coincided with that time and its demands. Robert Busnardo, who had almost as many run-ins with teachers as he did with fellow students, still got it right when, fifty years later, he found the right adjective to describe those Seabrook and Bridgeton educators of the middle decades of the twentieth century: "Giving. I think that's the word. Giving. They gave. The teachers gave something. I mean my teachers gave so much."

What teachers and administrators gave a lot of, in addition to lessons in the traditional subjects, was respect—respect for a child regardless of the child's color, native language, appearance, or class standing. One of those persons who, according to teachers who served during his administration, was happily in the right place at the right time was M. Gregg Hibbs, a Quaker, who was Bridgeton's superintendent of schools. When editors of the 1945 high school yearbook, the *Baconian,* asked him to write a few words for inclusion in that year's edition, the first to include Japanese American students, he gave them these lines that first offered truth and then wise counsel to the graduates: "Happiness and peace follow respect for the rights of all creeds, all races, all peoples. Teach that concept throughout your life." Hibbs's counterpart at Seabrook School was Elizabeth F. Moore, who served as principal there for most of the thirty-two years she spent in Upper Deerfield. The old Seabrook School now bears her name. "What a principal she was," remembers Marion Moore (no relation), who was a student and later a teacher during Elizabeth Moore's long tenure. Miss Moore was a strict disciplinarian who might be called overcontrolling today. But the stern disciplinarian had a soft spot for children who needed help. Albert Johnson, who had Miss Moore as an eighth-grade teacher in 1935 (she continued teaching that grade until she retired as principal in 1959), remembers the day when she approached his desk and said, "'Albert, you're not doing well in handwriting' [penmanship was important at that time]. Then she sat down and showed me what I was doing wrong and how I could improve. All the students responded well to her because they knew she cared and would help them." In thirty-two years, she never missed a day when school was open, not because of sickness, not because of weather, and, of course, not because she just needed a day off. "She made the school what it was," Marion Moore said. If the teachers were kind and respectful, as Robert Busnardo noted, it was because Miss Moore encouraged them to be kind and respectful. "She was a unique individual"—another person perfectly matched to her time and place.

However, it is entirely conceivable, perhaps even reasonable to expect, that Elizabeth Moore and the teachers who served under her would be overwhelmed when the Seabrook School population doubled and then tripled with children from so many different lands and cultures (classrooms were added in 1945 and 1948). After all, Miss Moore came to Seabrook School in 1927, four years after it opened, when most of the children who attended the school then could trace their ancestry to British-born colonists who had come south from Connecticut in the late seventeenth and early eighteenth centuries. They had come, as noted by Alan Palmer, "in search of good soil, a warmer climate and . . . freedom of worship." Up until the 1920s in rural Cumberland County "there was little, if any, uniform standard of teaching quality maintained [and] any high school graduate could get a teaching certificate by passing an examination conducted by the county superintendent of schools."[6] How could a school administrator from that simple—some might say backward—epoch be so successful coinciding with the children who lived in the exploding global village of the 1940s and 1950s? "She adapted well." That is the terse explanation offered by Doris Kennedy, who served as business administrator for the Upper Deerfield School District just before Miss Moore's retirement.

And Miss Moore did more than adapt. Instead of insisting that every student adhere to the local, ingrained WASP culture prevalent in that corner of southern New Jersey, she chose to teach students first to value their own culture and then to learn about and respect other cultures—for example, the one that nurtured the boy in the last row who spoke Estonian, or another that formed the girl whose parents were born in Japan. "Miss Moore made sure that all the children were exposed to each culture and each nationality that came in," recalled Marion Moore. School assembly programs, for instance, featured music and dance representing different cultures. Often, it was the children themselves who performed: perhaps Joe Franco singing an Italian song or the little girl whose parents came from Holland dancing in wooden shoes. Students sometimes learned the music or dance of another country by trying it out for themselves. Shirley Stotz Pillow vividly remembers May Day 1948. "I was in a Japanese dance with my Japanese friends. The kimono was so extremely tight that it was hard to breathe. Five of us were wearing bobby socks and saddle shoes while the other five girls had the proper footwear." On other occasions, the Japanese Minyo Dancers or the Estonian Choir, all adults, would appear on stage. "I remember a Japanese man who came to play the koto [a stringed instrument] for the children. I don't know where he came from. Miss Moore would bring in different people."[7]

Teaching about various cultures and encouraging respect for each was a staple in every classroom. Olive Dougherty came to Seabrook School in 1954 to teach second grade. She had taught elsewhere for eleven years but always wanted to work at Seabrook School because of what she had heard about the interesting mix of students and because of Miss Moore and her emphasis on learning about different lands and peoples and their customs. At first she had been reluctant to apply for a position at Seabrook School. "I knew Miss Moore had such high standards; I didn't know if I could meet them. When I told her that, she laughed and said, 'Why didn't you come here ten years ago?'"

Dougherty's great love had always been social studies, so the variety of students in her classroom was made to order. Her lessons on peoples of the world climaxed each year with the Christmas Program. Students would divide into villages representing different countries; they studied the history of each country, its flag, and its money. "I always had money from all the countries, and the children would learn a carol from each country. On my classroom door I had a Christmas tree that the children cut out, and I would have on each limb a different language. The top one was always Japanese, because it was a single character and fit neatly on the peak of the tree. The first year, Mr. Susaski, who was the custodian, came up to me and whispered quietly, 'Mrs. Dougherty, I hate to tell you, but the character is upside down.'"

Of the thirty-eight children in her class, nearly half were newly arrived from foreign countries; many of the others were Japanese Americans, Italian Americans, Jamaicans, and children whose parents came from Appalachia. Sometimes an immigrant child hurrying to become an American would turn against his or her native culture. Dougherty would not allow that to happen. "I had a boy and girl who were half Russian, and they used to bring in beautiful artifacts and books written in Russian for show and tell. [Dougherty and her husband traveled the world, and she herself always had something for show and tell.] All at once I saw nothing from the boy and girl. I asked them why they had stopped bringing in things. 'We're not proud to be Russians,' they said. 'It's not popular here now.' [The Cold War was frigid just then.] It really put a damper on them, so it was my job to pull them out of that." To meet this challenge, Dougherty didn't really do anything new. Routinely, she had had the children count to twenty in a different language each day, and she had never stressed one nationality in relation to another. However, for a while, she perhaps emphasized Russia and the Russian language just a little more until the Russian children began bringing in their artifacts again. "The boy, Victor Kowlenko, told me later that I had made him proud again to be Russian."

Dougherty visited the home of every child in her classroom. "I was always welcomed, especially in the homes of Europeans. They made a big fuss over a teacher, you know. There [in Europe] a teacher was *somebody.* I remember a Latvian boy I had in class; he was tall and as blonde as he could be. One day I got a sympathy card from his mother. She thought he had misbehaved in class and she felt sorry for me. I was surprised, because the boy had not misbehaved." In addition to visiting students' homes, Dougherty had students to her home. When it came time for field trips in the spring, other classes might go to the zoo in Cape May or Philadelphia, but her students chose to come to her house. She would show them the many curios and artifacts she and her husband had collected from around the world, most of which were too large to bring in for show and tell. She also had a collection of more than 100 dolls. After the house tour, Dougherty and the children would have a cookout in the backyard.

Not only did Olive Dougherty and other teachers take full advantage of the melting pot that bubbled in their classrooms, but Miss Moore made sure that the cafeteria was also involved in culture sharing. It was here that many children tasted food of other countries for the first time. Unless a child was sick or allergic to an ingredient in the food, he or she was expected—required—to eat whatever the cooks had prepared for the day. Every child had to take some of whatever was being served, whether or not he or she ate it all. "Back in those days [1940s], there were many different things tried," Marion Moore recalled of her days at the school. "I'll never forget when they made spinach soup. It was a first. Since Seabrook Farms grew lots of spinach, Miss Moore decided all the children should have spinach soup."

Students also had an opportunity to try different foods in their classrooms. Kenneth Hill, whose family came from Tennessee, remembers the teachers being very sensitive to the ethnic backgrounds of students. "The first time I ever had a mango was at school, because some of the kids [primarily the Jamaicans] ate them all the time and we had never heard of them. We tried everything. The Germans brought in different foods for us. We had some Estonians who brought their food. The Japanese, the Cubans, they were all there [with their ethnic food.] And the southerners, like me, we took in some corn bread. Some of the kids had never eaten corn bread before." Food tasting was part of a lesson, not simply inserted somewhere in the school day to take a break from arithmetic. "We were trying to learn about each other," Hill said. "We knew we were all different, but yet it didn't matter. We all had that kind of bond and wanted to learn. Everyone got along, you see; that was the thing that was so impressive. Going to school was like going to the United Nations every day."

At the United Nations in New York, of course, delegates and visitors are able to understand what is going on because batteries of men and women sit at microphones and instantly translate

Japanese into German, or Russian into Spanish, or Chinese into English. All that the delegates and visitors need do is turn on a headset to the language of their choice. At Seabrook School, Miss Moore and the teachers made English the language of everybody's choice, as there was no one to translate lessons into Estonian, German, Russian, Polish, or Latvian. Furthermore, classes labeled "English as a Second Language" or "Bilingual Instruction" did not exist in the 1940s and 1950s. L. William Morris was a student teacher at Seabrook School in 1951 and 1952 and returned in 1961 as chief school administrator, a position he held until 1991. In an interview shortly before his death in 2001, he said Seabrook School never offered formal or special instruction in the English language to students arriving from Europe. "They just picked it up. It's surprising, but we always had the philosophy that any child who came [to the school] became part of a buddy system in which [other] kids kind of took him under their wings. And I think teachers became very friendly [with children who did not speak English] and allowed for the language barrier. Believe it or not, it only took a matter, in most cases, of just a few months and they were speaking English well, and I would say that within a year or two they were speaking it quite fluently, [depending on] the intelligence level of the child."

Although the school did not offer English instruction during the school year, some children fresh from the displaced persons camps learned basic English during the summer months in classes conducted at Community House. The Reverend Toomas Vaga remembers a beginners and an advanced class in English offered at Community House during the summer of 1949 when he arrived with his parents at age eleven; immigrants who arrived in the early 1950s, however, do not recall such instruction being offered. His first encounter with English came soon after he and his family disembarked from the ship that brought them from Germany. They were standing on the dock waiting for their luggage when a Port Authority policeman came up to young Toomas. "He asked me what we were doing there; I sort of understood him and he sort of understood me." Toomas was placed in the advanced class that summer of 1949 because he had been taught some English while attending school in a displaced persons camp. Helgi Malleus Viire also recalls English instruction being available for Estonian children during the summer (before the arrival of the *volksdeutsche* in the early 1950s), but she did not go to the classes. "I just learned from school and being around American children, because on the playground we needed to communicate in English. The process was difficult for me because I was very shy and I did not [readily] join in children's games." Eventually, her family moved from Hoover Village to 988 Juniper Street in the federal housing originally built for the Japanese Americans. "We lived on a corner next door to an American family from the South, the Hendersons. They had five children, and that is where I learned [most] of my English, both good and bad." The Hendersons also introduced her to onion sandwiches: two slices of white bread, butter, and slices of sweet onion. "And lots of salt. We all ate them so we could get along real well. We didn't care much about how we smelled when we talked to each other. We were all alike."

Learning English by picking it up from other children, teachers, friends, comic books, and movies was difficult for two reasons. First, children who were still struggling to learn the new language often missed key instructions from their teacher and became embarrassed. Second, when they went home, their parents generally conversed in their native language. "When I got to Seabrook School, Miss Moore put me in the third grade, and the teacher there was so tired of having people that didn't speak English," remembers Erik Kohv. "It was hard, you know. You didn't understand anything [the teachers] were saying. I mean you didn't even understand when it was time to leave." Roman Czelada spoke Ukrainian, Polish, Russian, and a little German, but not much English. "The rules were hard to understand," he said. "I mean there were times when I did things that I wasn't supposed to. [For example,] we weren't supposed to ride our bikes on the playground at school. I did that a couple of times [because I didn't know the rules] and got into trouble with Miss Moore. One of the hardest things was getting used to social etiquette. People might say one thing [in English] and it could have two or three different meanings [depending on] the way it was said and facial expressions." Erhardt Wagner, whose parents were German, doesn't remember having any bad experiences at school, but when he went home and his parents spoke only German, he had trouble keeping ideas and information straight in his head. "I was kind of thinking backward," he said.

Reet Sikkemae's Estonian family arrived at Seabrook Farms two weeks before summer vacation from school, so Miss Moore strongly suggested that her parents place Reet in a summer class for English instruction. "When I saw the other kids get on a school bus in front of the Community House to go to Day Camp [sponsored by Community House] at Parvin State Park, while we were inside learning English, I swore I was going to learn it so well that I would never be deprived of my summer fun again. And I did learn it so well that later in school I was asked to explain grammar to kids who could not understand the teacher's explanation."[8]

The adults of the various ethnic communities that existed side by side in the global village tried very hard to guard and preserve their own cultures. It wasn't easy, because Seabrook School and Bridgeton High School became giant mixers in which a white child from the segregated South might become best friends with a black child from Barbados, or a Ukrainian girl whose mother and father spoke only Russian at home might spend time after school with a boy whose parents emigrated from Italy. Reet Sikkemae proves the point.

> At school, everything was okay, but at home it was a different matter. To be tolerant and enjoy the diversity . . . was the purpose of us living in a community like Seabrook. My favorite playmates were Japanese kids. I also liked the German kids, but I stayed on the fringe of my own [Estonian] ethnic group. Unlike our parents, I did not believe we would ever return to Estonia, so I didn't see any point in keeping to my ethnic group. The old songs and the dancing were beautiful, but each ethnic event was like a funeral—things will never be [the same] again. On the one hand, I wanted to keep to the cultural heritage, but at ethnic events I found it extremely painful to watch the older people cry, so I stayed away more and more. There was just too much pain associated with the past. The other cultures didn't affect me the same way; hence, my interest in all others more than my own.[9]

Yet the adults wanted it both ways. They certainly expected their children to succeed in school and to grow strong and straight in the fresh soil of America, but they did not want their children to cut themselves off from the old roots. Rei R. Noguchi stated the case for the adults:

> By most accounts, Seabrook School, one of the highest-rated public schools in New Jersey in the 1950s, succeeded in instilling basic skills and knowledge in its diverse body of students. Many Seabrook School graduates later went on to excel in the classrooms at Bridgeton High School. Indeed, because of the success of Seabrook School in instilling the new—and, in the process, Americanizing the young—the task of preserving the old proved much more difficult. In [the] face of great odds, parents turned to religious organizations and social clubs in an effort to preserve ethnic languages and traditions.[10]

From the early 1950s, the children from the global village arguably had a greater impact on the intellectual and social life at Bridgeton High School than did the boom in science education launched by Sputnik and the emotional fervor caused by Elvis. "In 1962, Seabrook School provided approximately twenty percent of the students at Bridgeton Senior High School, yet six of the ten seniors graduating with 'highest distinction' that year were graduates of Seabrook School; in that same year, Seabrook School graduates served as presidents of the senior class, honor society, science club, [and] debating club; editor of the school newspaper; as well as captains of the boys' varsity football, basketball, baseball and tennis teams and girls' varsity field hockey and basketball teams."[11] Frank Mastoraki, whose ethnic roots are Greek, taught history and economics at the high school from 1947 to 1961. In a speech delivered at the celebration of Seabrook's fiftieth year, October 9, 1994, he said, "I wondered [at first] how the students would handle my strange last name. That issue was resolved when

I soon learned my name was as easy to pronounce as Fukuyama, Yokoyama, Hasuike, [and] Nishimura." Mastoraki retrieved "roll books with their mildew and musty smell to review the names of the students in [his] classes" for a speech he gave on the occasion of the fiftieth anniversary of the arrival of the first contingent of Japanese Americans at Seabrook Farms. "I truly had multi-ethnic classes. I marveled [that] with the exception of four, all of the Japanese American students in my classes from 1947 to 1961 earned A's and B's, and there were very few B's. Either I was very easy or they were very smart. Of course, it had to be the latter."

The Estonians arrived after the Japanese Americans, and there grew an unstated and perhaps even unrealized, but nevertheless genuine, competition between the two groups of students for top scholastic honors. Parents of both sets of students had been helpless to prevent their own educational pursuits and life goals from being forcibly snatched from them, and they came to Seabrook with little more than pride in past accomplishments and hope for their own and, more important, their children's future. The Japanese American students had the advantage of growing up in this country and knowing the language and customs of America. Estonian students also had an advantage. Although many of their parents had told interrogators at the displaced persons camps that they had had farming experience, very few actually had; many had earned college degrees in Estonia and had worked in the professions. Both sets of parents, however, were intent on their children excelling in high school and going on to college. And nearly all did.

June graduation ceremonies at Bridgeton High School in the middle part of the twentieth century were eagerly anticipated by the residents of Cumberland County, nearly as much as by graduating seniors, their parents, and teachers. Frank Mastoraki was almost certainly correct when he observed, "There probably was nothing quite like those ceremonies in the whole state"—or perhaps anywhere else in rural America. To call them ceremonies, however, is like calling the Christmas pageant at Radio City Music Hall in New York just another theater show. What happened each June in the high school stadium was nothing short of a spectacle—an extravaganza. Under the expert direction of Catherine Loder, whose everyday cover was curriculum coordinator, the football field was transformed into a giant stage where students performed in a series of elaborate and colorful tableaus that featured music and dance from many nations and cultures. Mastoraki said, "The emphasis was on ethnicity. Miss Loder promoted the idea that people need to get to know each other, to accept people who are different from [themselves]." Just as they did at Seabrook School assemblies, students in the commencement day productions often played roles in a tableau representing a culture other than their own. In his speech at the celebration of Seabrook's fiftieth year, Mastoraki recalled: "It wasn't unusual, for example, to see Japanese Americans performing a Mexican hat dance."

The graduating class of 1945 included Japanese American students for the first time, and their yearbook, the *Baconian,* displayed their pictures: Frank Tokeski—"Hails from sunny California . . . enjoys a good football game . . . notice that dimple"; Alice Nakagawa—"California bombshell"; Edward (Eddie) Kato—"Math and music right down his line"; Shigeko (Shig) Sakabe—"A model stenographer . . . also a model . . . warm interest in those about her"; George Murashige—"A gentleman of speed from the Pacific coast . . . basketball star." The ceremony that year took place on June 6, the first anniversary of D day, and students and audience alike wrapped themselves in blankets to protect themselves from unexpected and unwanted snow flurries. The commencement program featured a Seabrook Farms ad that promoted "F for Victory: Faith, Firepower, Fortitude and [of course] Food." The theme for the spectacle was "This Is My Country: The History of America in Tableaus," and the chorus members included seven Japanese American students. The next day's edition of the *Bridgeton Evening News* reported the commencement on page one opposite this headline: "450 Superforts Lay Bombs on Osaka."[12]

Liina Keerdoja had come from Estonia to the global village as a little girl. She looked back from the distance of fifty years on the experience she had shared with hundreds of other children from displaced and uprooted families who attended Seabrook School and Bridgeton High School and wrote new chapters in the history of rural America. "We children found ourselves readily interacting with children of other backgrounds. We learned together, played together, occasionally got into fights together, and in the process came to regard one another's different cultural and ethnic backgrounds not as something negative, but as the most normal and natural thing in the world."[13]

In September 1945, when many of the June graduates of Bridgeton High School were entering the college campuses and World War II had officially and mercifully ended on the deck of the battleship *Missouri* in Tokyo Bay, Seabrook Farms looked to a promising and prosperous postwar future. "Food is as essential in peacetime as in war," began an editorial in that month's issue of *The Seabrooker.*

> Many food consumers have developed a taste for quick-frozen vegetables and fruits. But the number of consumers who demand quick-frozen foods in neighborhood markets today is small compared to those who will do so five years from now. In other words, the quick-frozen industry is still an "infant." It will grow to man's estate with a speed to make the head spin with the elimination of wartime controls that prevented manufacture of refrigeration cabinets. Once such cabinets are easily obtained, virtually every food store in the United States will stock frozen foods. All this points toward certain skyrocketing of the total amount consumers will spend for frozen foods each year. Now a $200,000,000 industry, frozen foods unquestionably will hit the billion dollar mark [soon.] Thus, employees of Seabrook Farms . . . can look toward an economically secure future.[14]

Unfortunately, what the writer of the editorial had not seen in his crystal ball was competition. By 1952, frozen food packers were popping up faster than dandelions in a spring lawn, particularly on the West Coast. However, it wasn't so much a case of the new companies cutting into Seabrook Farms' sales in stores, because the quality of Seabrook Farms frozen foods was generally far superior to that of the newcomers' products; the real problem was that they were cutting big slices out of the money pie—the pool of bank loans that seasonal operations like frozen foods processors depended on. Jack Seabrook, then executive vice president of the company, was witness to the turmoil. "[The] new producers with uncertain quality created a situation that began to alarm their Eastern financial backers. Some big New York banks with little knowledge of the frozen foods business had extended easy credit to the new packers. In particular, these banks did not know that top-quality foods can almost always be sold at some price, but when there is a surplus, poor quality is difficult or impossible to sell. Carloads of frozen broccoli and other crops arrived in New York from California in 1952–53. Sometimes [the food] could not be sold to cover the cost of the freight alone." Seabrook Farms, as always, relied heavily on short-term loans needed to pay expenses at the start of a growing season and then paid off with profits from sales in the fall and winter. Now, however, that system common and crucial to the business had broken down. "These [short-term] loans were never paid off since much of the money raised as short-term working capital loans actually went into capital spending for the plant. With some banks now in a panic about the glut of frozen foods and with selling prices dropping, our own banks became very uneasy and began to press for repayment. With the company's finances balanced so precariously on a mountain of long overdue short-term loans, the thought of the potential consequence was sobering to all concerned. Wild rumors spread quickly, but those who knew what actually had happened tried to calm the key employees."[15]

Jack Seabrook became president of Seabrook Farms in 1954, although seventy-three-year-old C. F. remained as chief executive officer. "It was obvious the plant and the bloated workforce were too big for our sales capacity," Jack Seabrook wrote. "Despite our struggle to sell more, inventory had been piling up since 1951. Unit costs were higher than the competition's. These problems had all been suspected for several years, but C. F. refused to acknowledge them." He blamed the "bloated workforce" in part on C. F.'s recruiting of *volksdeutsche* in the early 1950s. In any event, in 1955 he set out to reduce the number of employees. "Downsizing was not easy, but it was made possible because no one's favorites pets were spared. In addition to the obvious fat, such as make-work jobs for favorites and questionable jobs like the [Deerfield Presbyterian]

Church organist, a lot of useful but nonessential departments were swept away. These included the climatology research lab, the photographic department, [and] the social service organization, among others. We tried to cushion the layoff pain for long-time employees by having them do 'detail' work in large retail frozen-food departments under the direction of our sales force. C. F. was enthusiastic, even helpful at first, but, as more people complained to him about the changes, by 1956 he began to make bitter remarks about running the company to suit the bankers."[16]

In a February 1957 report to growers (farmers under contract to Seabrook Farms), Jack Seabrook called attention to progress and benefits (a "new sales record of $27 million" and a "larger share of the retail food dollar" going to growers), but also pointed out that competition was still fierce, causing "a decline in industry selling prices." He tried to be upbeat at the end of the report: "1956 was a record year for growers if a difficult one for processors. Your awareness of our problems helps us both to succeed. We must both mold production plans in 1957 to fit marketing requirements and consumer preferences. Together we can continue to keep our little segment of American agriculture strong and healthy."

Although Seabrook Farms and the residents of the global village had a few great years ahead, C. F. did not, and before he died in 1964, he alone gravely wounded and nearly killed the argi-industry he had given birth to in 1913.

Chapter 8

"So Long, Seabrook"

On Wednesday, March 31, 1982, the *Bridgeton Evening News* marked an important occasion with its page one headline, "So Long, Seabrook." The article continued: "The last ninety-seven workers . . . will collect their final paycheck today."[1] Although the newspaper noted the official time of death for Seabrook Farms (known then as Seabrook Foods), the death knell had first sounded on the night of May 16, 1959. It was on this date that C. F.—aged, probably suffering from senility to some degree, and most certainly furious at his son Jack for changing the way the Old Man had run things for a half century—agreed to sell his controlling shares in Seabrook Farms Company. Seeman Brothers, the buyer, was a wholesale grocery company that had enjoyed an excellent reputation before being taken over by what Jack described as a "shadowy group headed nominally by a man named Jim Fowler." What Seeman Brothers purchased were the processing and freezing plants, the cold storage warehouse, and other buildings pertaining to the operation of the freezing and packing operation. C. F. still retained ownership of the housing units that constituted what was left of the global village and considerable farm acreage.[2]

In the same month that Seeman Brothers took control, the new management published a message of reassurance to employees, growers, suppliers, and customers in *The Seabrooker,* the company newsletter: "The policies which have been responsible for the growth of this company will be continued. All employees will retain their jobs; local growers will keep on supplying produce; customers will receive the same high quality and services. . . . We are sure that the association . . . with Seeman Brothers will result in greater markets, increased buying from local producers, and greater stability of employment at the Seabrook Farms plant."[3]

The message turned out to be worse than boilerplate. Jack Seabrook was suspicious of Fowler and his group from the beginning. "Whether Fowler was just incompetent or all along intended to loot the company, or both, I cannot say. The company went downhill, gradually at first, and then rapidly. The new Fowler management was not especially interested in crops grown in New Jersey, and the Seabrook plant was eventually relegated to merely repacking frozen produce grown, processed, and frozen elsewhere."[4] So much for the new owners' promise to local growers. Seeman Brothers finally sold the business to Spring Mills, Inc., primarily a textile firm headquartered in South Carolina, which operated the plant until it no longer proved profitable. That March day in 1982 is when Spring Mills made this determination.

That C. F. should choose spring of 1959 to gravely wound the baby he had nurtured into robust adulthood is particularly regrettable inasmuch as Seabrook Farms at that time "was making good money, sales were up sharply, bank loans were down. The Board of Directors was studying the acquisition by lease or by purchase of three small frozen food plants, one each in Georgia, Idaho and California."[5] Jack Seabrook attributes C. F.'s actions primarily to two factors: First, the Old Man was senile and second, he "had lost touch" with what was happening to the frozen food business in which he had been a worldwide pioneer. He only implies a third factor, which may have been even more important than the other two. For at least the first half of the twentieth century, C. F. *was* Seabrook Farms: Its very existence was due to his ingenuity, his energy, his grittiness. Although his three sons, once they had matured, were vital to the business, it wasn't until the latter half of the century that they increasingly exerted control until *they* became Seabrook Farms. Perhaps, then, C. F. dealt Seabrook Farms the fatal blow in 1959 as a desperate but defiant reminder to his sons, and to anyone else who mattered, that the Old Man was still the Old Man.

When Seeman Brothers management printed its open letter, there were fewer than 2,000 employees working in the plant to read it. At its prime in the 1940s and early 1950s, the plant's workforce during the summer months numbered as many as 4,000. The attrition was due primarily to the big sweep conducted by Jack Seabrook in 1954 and 1955 and to voluntary relocation on a grand scale by many of those families who had come to work at Seabrook Farms between 1944 and 1952. Not a few Seabrook Farms workers, when they chose or were forced to leave the security and interrelatedness to which they had become accustomed in the global village, confronted an uncertain and sometimes hostile future. With the end of World War II, for example, the West Coast was no longer forbidden to Japanese Americans, and a number returned to the hometowns where they had been rounded up by their government in the spring of 1942 and shipped off to internment camps. Unfortunately, these were not always happy homecomings, because some returnees found that their houses, farms, or businesses had been confiscated or allowed to deteriorate. They also encountered residual prejudice. The late Ellen Nakamura, who was one of the first Japanese Americans to come to Seabrook and later served as president of the Seabrook Educational and Cultural Center, recalled in the fall of 1994, on the occasion of the fiftieth anniversary of the Japanese Americans arrival in the global village, that by the late 1940s, the Japanese Americans began to leave in droves. "I said to myself [at the time] everybody must hate this place where I staked my life." In 1993, however, she had discovered that her assumption was not true. She attended a reunion of Japanese Americans in Los Angeles that year and learned from attendees that most of them retained favorable memories of Seabrook.

Although Japanese Americans were at least able to return to a familiar land and people, the Peruvian Japanese, who were not permitted to reenter Peru until after 1950, were at a greater disadvantage if they left the global village that had become familiar and comfortable, even if the work had been hard and tiresome in the extreme. Seiichi Higashide and his family are a case in point. He was one of those people who left Seabrook voluntarily as soon as he convinced himself that he could find more fulfilling, going-somewhere employment to replace his unfulfilling, going-nowhere job at Seabrook Farms. He had immigrated to Peru from Japan in 1930 and had become a successful businessperson. After Pearl Harbor, he was among the first Peruvian Japanese to be targeted for removal from Peru and interned by the United States government at Crystal City, Texas. In September 1946 he and his wife and five children joined approximately 300 other Peruvian Japanese who accepted an invitation from Seabrook Farms. They were to work at Seabrook along with the 2,000-plus mainland Japanese Americans, most of whom had already arrived. A sixth child was born to the family at Seabrook. Like almost every other working adult in the global village, Higashide immediately found that life could be very hard:

> On the fourth day after we arrived at Seabrook, we came face-to-face with the realities that confronted us. My wife and I were assigned to work at the frozen food factory on different shifts. Except for the winter months, the factory operated continuously, twenty-four hours a day. The changeover between the day shift and the night shift was at 6 A.M. and 6 P.M. We were required to work twelve hours a day. We had only one free day every two weeks, when we moved from one shift to another. There were no paid holidays, no sick leave.
>
> As we entered our third year at Seabrook [1948], our lives had become fully settled and we could, to a certain degree, gain some perspective of our future there. If

> we stayed, our family would not be faced with basic survival. In the future, we might leave the company's living quarters, rent an apartment in Bridgeton, buy a car, and enjoy a simple American lifestyle. As long as we continued our relationship with Seabrook Farms, however, we could not look forward to much more than that. We would not be able, as we had when we started our business in [Peru], to dream of broader possibilities. We were mainly concerned about the future of our children. They would be able to finish high school at Seabrook, but if they were to continue their education further, we almost certainly would have to move on quickly to establish a basis for other opportunities. As we entered our third year at Seabrook, I began to consider ways to escape the dead end that was our situation in Seabrook.[6]

Higashide's plan of action called for a move to a large city, where his business management skills honed in Peru might stand a better chance of being welcomed and utilized. He ruled out nearby Philadelphia, as well as New York and Baltimore, because he had no contact there and because he and his wife, both issei, still spoke English poorly. However, he had kept in touch with Kunio Takeshita, a single man, who had left Seabrook some time earlier and moved to Chicago. Single men and couples without children were often the first to test the waters outside the safe harbor of Seabrook Village. He decided to go to Chicago alone in December 1948 to "check out the possibilities there with my own eyes." His friend lived on the near north side of Chicago and worked in a factory; he arranged for Higashide to take a part-time job on the night shift at the plant. Takeshita's studio apartment was small and in a neighborhood that must have resembled the Seabrook global village, because, Higashide said, "many different ethnic groups lived in a bewildering variety of cultural behaviors." He found another apartment in the same building consisting of two rooms, one twelve-by-fifteen feet and the other twelve-by-twelve. The smaller room contained a kitchen of sorts.

Surprisingly, Higashide concluded that these cramped quarters would suffice temporarily for his family of eight.

When he arrived back at Seabrook, his Japanese American friends tried to dissuade him from going off to Chicago where he had no promise of permanent employment and where the family's living space would be smaller than that at Seabrook. He quoted the advice of neighbors: "You should give it up, Higashide," they told him. "Chicago is very different from Seabrook. First of all, it would place your children in a pitiful situation. Here, we have farms and open spaces and almost all the workers are Japanese. If you go to Chicago, it won't be the same. You don't know what to expect. Chicago is a city of mobsters. If you go to such a place, how would your family with six children survive?" Higashide disregarded the counsel, and in January 1949 the family left for Chicago and was welcomed there by the typically Chicagoan "biting north winds." Very soon the words of warning spoken earlier by friends at Seabrook haunted Higashide and his wife. "Our first two or three years in Chicago were a time of complete and ultimate poverty. We did not have stable jobs; we did not have a real home for our family; we did not have fluency in English. In everything, it seemed, we were lacking." Eventually, the Higashides earned a fairly comfortable living managing rental properties, and they spent their later years in Hawaii near their son Arthur.[7]

Workers actively recruited by Seabrook Farms, which, of course, included nearly everyone other than longtime local residents, agreed to stay at least six months. The majority of workers remained much longer, many until retirement or until forced out by reductions in the workforce. Among those persons hired late in Seabrook Farms' prime and who left early were some of the displaced persons from the Baltic states, primarily Estonians. Many of the Estonians, both men and women, had either earned a college degree in their homeland before the war or had at least completed some level of higher education. A number had worked as professionals in Estonia. Therefore, the tedious, mind-numbing work in Seabrook's plants was especially unappealing to them, even though nearly all of the Estonians, in company with others who had come to Seabrook Farms with nothing more than a glimmer of hope, labored long and uncomplainingly. "As the months passed [after arriving at Seabrook], most of the Estonians displayed a remarkable ability to adapt to the new environment. Living in the barracks, at the most, lasted one or two years [before many families moved into the small houses of West Village]. During that time, some Estonians started to leave Seabrook Farms to look for better paying jobs in other cities. Some found employment with construction companies as carpenters or bricklayers. Many found jobs in banks and insurance offices."[8]

Approximately 300 families who came to work at Seabrook Farms in the 1940s and early 1950s still live in the immediate area. However, as one would expect, most of the children of those men and women who worked the never-ending and monotonous hours at Seabrook Farms left the global village at the first opportunity. Their parents not only encouraged their flight, they made it possible. "For most Seabrook parents of the 1940s and 1950s, working long hours at the Seabrook Farms factory left little time to further their own formal schooling. Typically, parents sacrificed their own education and career ambitions for the education of their children. The Seabrook Japanese American community has shown a high rate of students continuing their education. A 1958 news article in the Philadelphia *Evening Bulletin* reported that, since settling in Seabrook [beginning in 1944], the Japanese American community sent every one of its children to high school and every one graduated, with three-quarters going on to college."[9] What was true of the offspring of the Japanese Americans was also true of the children of other Seabrook employees, particularly the Estonians. "The first and foremost goal for Estonian parents was to provide their children with an education. To acquire a college education soon became the rule rather than the exception among young Seabrook Estonians. At least eighty-five percent earned college degrees, including seventeen Ph.D.s and twenty-one master's degrees."[10]

The list of children of Seabrook workers who benefited greatly from the sacrifices made by their parents is a long one. Therefore, only a few of the post-Seabrook lives of the second generation are sketched here as examples.

◆ JUHAN SIMONSON

As a student at Bridgeton High School in the early 1950s, he usually knew the answers to the questions asked by his history teacher, but he was too self-conscious about his Estonian accent to raise his hand. He later earned his bachelor's degree from Rutgers, the state university, and a master's degree in regional and city planning, then a relatively new field, from the University of Pennsylvania. Simonson served New Jersey as a planning coordinator and later as director of the new Office of Ethnic Affairs. For many years, he served as president of the Estonian American National Council.

◆ MICHI NISHIURA WEGLYN

At one point, she was taken off the plant assembly line to act as a disc jockey, which meant she was supposed to play marches and other rousing music over the loudspeaker system to wake up workers who were dozing off at the tail end of an endlessly boring shift. When she and the workers got fed up with Sousa et al, she slipped in some Perry Como records. Years later, she became the head costume designer for the *Perry Como Show,* as well as for other television and Broadway productions. In 1976, the University of Washington Press published Weglyn's story of the Japanese American internment during World War II, *Years of Infamy,* which, she reported, the *New York Times* called "fascinating and shattering . . . extraordinary history."

◆ DONNA PEARSON

She is the daughter of Samah and Eula Pearson. Her father was Jamaican, and her mother was one of the African American college students employed at Seabrook during the summer months in the early years of World War II. Her father was the liaison between management and the hundreds of workers from the West Indies, and both her parents became active in local politics. "I went to Bridgeton High School with a lot of children from Seabrook, so we had a very good mix. Just growing up with different cultures, you have a different attitude about life," she said. Today Pearson is a member of the Cumberland County Board of Freeholders, the county's governing body.[11]

◆ KENNETH HILL

Other workers at Seabrook Farms referred to his parents as "hillbillies." They and hundreds of other families had been recruited in the down-and-out towns stretching along the base of the Appalachian range in Tennessee. His father, Rufus, left before the rest of the family, taking two days to drive north in a Model A Ford with a friend who had chipped in to buy the used car. Kenneth Hill was born in Bridgeton, and for much of his adult life he has served either as mayor or deputy mayor of Upper Deerfield Township. He also is president of the Seabrook Educational and Cultural Center. Today when Hill sees news stories on television about the blood shed by Israelis and Palestinians, and by Protestants and Catholics in Northern Ireland, he wonders why people can't get along with each other. "We did here at Seabrook, get along, I mean."

◆ VALLO TRUUMEES

He served two years as an Army officer in Vietnam. While stationed in Binh Khe, he helped build and furnish an elementary school for Vietnamese children, aided by donations of money and materials from Seabrook workers and gifts of books and toys from the children of Seabrook School, which he had attended as a child. "Even after more than twenty-five years, I can clearly recall the joy on the faces of those children," he wrote in 1996. Truumees retired as a colonel, having won two Bronze Stars, three Air Medals, and the Vietnamese Cross of Gallantry.[12]

◆ SEIKI MURONO

Born to Peruvian Japanese parents while they were incarcerated at Crystal City, Texas, he and his family came to Seabrook in 1945. "Education was placed first and foremost. This was our ticket out of [Seabrook], toward a better life, and so we all strove to do our best in school." He graduated from Seabrook School and Bridgeton High School and then earned a bachelor's degree from Franklin and Marshall College and an M.B.A. from American University. Murono retired in 1995 as a senior vice president of the Chase Manhattan Bank.[13]

◆ MARET MAISTE

She was one of six children who, along with their father and mother, emigrated to America and Seabrook Farms from a displaced persons camp in Germany in 1949. She became interested in art at Bridgeton High School, where the subjects for her painting were, not surprisingly, farm scenes and the brightly costumed Estonian folk dancers who performed regularly in the global village. After graduating from Bridgeton High School, Maiste attended the Maryland Institute College of Art and the Rinehart School of Sculpture. She has exhibited her work in galleries and shows in Baltimore, New York, San Francisco, Toronto, and elsewhere. Her painting of two couples dressed in typical Estonian folk dance costumes hangs in the Seabrook Educational and Cultural Center Museum.

The global village of the first half of the twentieth century is no more. There are physical traces: Hoover Annex, the Italian Village, and the camps for the men from the West Indies have long since been torn down, but the cinder block apartments of the government housing project, and the little houses of West Village are still inhabited. The ethnic and cultural conglomeration that once defined Seabrook, however, has dwindled away with Seabrook Farms. The apartments that once housed a heady mix of Japanese Americans, Estonians, Latvians, Appalachian people, Germans, Poles, Russians, and others are now occupied almost exclusively by African American and Latino families. The global village was supposed to have had a very different future. In the early 1970s, C. F.'s estate sold all the company housing and several thousands of acres of farmland to Mark Watson and C. J. Achee. In March 1972 the two men "presented to the [Upper Deerfield] Township Committee a master plan for the development of its extensive holdings by the creation of a new town to be known as [Farmingtown], an 'Agri-City,' which would ultimately encompass 6,000 acres of Township land with an estimated population of more than 45,000 people. The project did not come to fruition for a number of reasons. The [men were] not able to attract industrial developers to the area, nor was existing transportation adequate to make an agri-city accessible to the larger urban centers."[14]

In the 1940s and 1950s, *multicuturalism* wasn't even a word; today, in the Seabrook School now named the Moore School to honor its beloved longtime principal, multiculturalism is included in the social studies curriculum defined by the New Jersey State Department of Education, and, as often as not, it is found at www.yahooligans.com—and, of course, in the fourth-grade classroom presided over by Louise Ogata.

Ogata is of the third generation whose parents and grandparents inhabited the global village in its heyday. Her grandfather, Kanhichi Taniguchi, married her grandmother, Harumi Oride, in Hiroshima on January 31, 1921. Later that same year, Japan sent a delegation to the Arms Limitation Conference in Washington, the Taniguchis embarked for California, and C. F. Seabrook told a reporter, "All my life I wanted to be a construction engineer." The Taniguchis, who were denied United States citizenship and therefore remained aliens, became tenant farmers and raised seven children. When World War II broke out, the family was herded together with all other issei and nisei and dispatched to internment camps; the Taniguchis were sent to Poston, Arizona. The family relocated to Seabrook Farms in 1945. Four years later their eldest daughter, Hatsumi, married Ben Tsutomu Ogata. The Ogatas are Louise's parents. Louise was born in Bridgeton in 1953, attended all grades at the Seabrook School, and graduated from Bridgeton High School. She returned to the Moore School (née Seabrook) as a teacher in 1976.

Ogata's students look up family roots on the Internet, but she begins the lessons on multiculturalism pretty much as the teachers of the 1940s and 1950s did—with the children themselves and what they know about their family trees. Although her students enjoy the exploration of genealogy, it is not as easy to dig up roots as it used to be. In the early and middle decades of the last century, the schoolchildren didn't have to look very far for a connection to the old country; it might be through their parents, but almost certainly, as in Ogata's case, through grandparents. Today, when Ogata first asks children about their family histories, her question is often answered with another question: "Do you mean by my dad or my step-dad?" Ogata has discovered that a number of children are not sure where they came from. "And many kids have no idea who their grandparents are. That connectedness I knew doesn't exist very much anymore." Still, a few of her students are quite sure about the nationality or culture of relatives. Nicolis Costanzo and Sergio Cirri know that their family roots are planted deep in Italian soil, and they once brought homemade pizza to class as proof of their origin; Ryan Griffith also knows, and he contributed Irish soda bread.

When she was in high school and college in the late 1960s and early 1970s, Ogata was more concerned about being accepted by and blending into Caucasian society. "Now I have more of an appreciation for my Japanese background; before, I never considered going to Japan, but now I think I might do that." Ogata may indeed someday visit the land of her ancestors, but for now she is helping to ensure that the Japanese culture brought to Seabrook by her grandparents and parents in the 1940s doesn't disappear from southern New Jersey like so many of the 2,500 Japanese Americans who once lived in the global village; she is a member of both the Minyo Dancers and the Hoh Daiko Drummers.

Not only is Ogata, at age forty-nine, doing her share to keep alive the centuries-old Japanese folk dancing, the tradition is also in the hands and feet of thirty-five-year-old Stefanie Pierce and her eight-year-old daughter, Danielle. Danielle is one of about ten girls, aged six to twelve, who were formed into a kind of junior version of the adult Minyo Dancers in January 2002 under the direction of Kyoko Ohara. Although Japanese Americans came to Seabrook beginning in 1944, it wasn't until 1974 that the Minyo Dancers Club was formed by a teacher from Japan who, at that time, visited the United States. He came every year to help found such clubs and to teach existing organizations new dances and taped music. From 1974 until just recently, he, and later a female successor, brought with them to Seabrook five new dances each year. "You can figure how many dances we have on a rack in the basement of the Buddhist Temple," said Laye Nagahiro, one of the adult dancers. "We've forgotten how to do most of them." According to Ohara, most of the costumes and implements used by the Minyo Dancers are still imported from Japan, including kimonos, slippers, fans, and *kachi-kachi,* which the dancers themselves call "clackers." The Seabrook adult Minyo Dancers have performed at Jimmy Carter's inaugural, at the Cherry Blossom Festival in Washington, at Fairmount Park celebrations in Philadelphia, and elsewhere. They are regulars at the annual Obon festival honoring ancestors at the Buddhist Temple on Northville Road in Upper Deerfield.

Stefanie Pierce and her daughter are fourth- and fifth-generation Japanese Americans, yonsei and gosei, respectively. Danielle's great-great-grandmother, Sue Shiyekesa Kubota, was born in Japan in 1891 and was fifty-four when she came to Seabrook Farms from the internment camp in Poston, Arizona. Her daughter, May Kubota Ikeda, came with her. June Ikeda Mick, Danielle's grandmother, was born in Bridgeton. Pierce had to explain about Seabrook Farms even before she knew very much about its history. She works for Owens & Minor, a medical supply company that was, until recently, headquartered in a building next to the old Seabrook Farms plant on Parsonage Road. "Sometimes visitors would ask about the area, for example about who built all those little houses across the street [the old West Village]," she told me. "But it has been only recently that I have learned very much about what life in the internment camps and at Seabrook Farms was really like. I never knew, for instance, how hard everyone worked at Seabrook Farms." While we were talking, she learned a little more. Tadashi Ohara, Kyoko's husband, joined us and told how it was to grow up as a child in the Arizona desert internment camp. "We [the internees] dug a swimming hole in the sand and diverted some water from a nearby canal that connected the camp to the Colorado River. But to get to the pool, kids had to run barefoot through the hot sand. To keep our feet from burning, we ran from the shelter of the buildings to a lone telephone pole, where we stood for a while in the cooler sand beneath the pole's shadow before making a run for the water."

Younger generations are often accused, and are sometimes actually guilty, of believing that history commenced at their birth and that legacy consists of whatever Grandma and Pop-pop left behind in their wills. The perceptions of cousins Toomas Truumees and Thomas and Andres Vilms are definitely exceptions to that half truth–half myth. All three young men made a point early in life to acquire a better understanding and appreciation for that piece of American history their Estonian parents and grandparents created at Seabrook Farms.

Truumees, age twenty-nine in 2002, who describes himself as a business entrepreneur, ventured into the past as a sixth-grader in Hopewell Township, the municipality where C. F. Seabrook also lived as a child and which abuts Upper Deerfield Township, the locale of Seabrook Farms. Not surprisingly, his sixth grade history project was the history of Seabrook Farms. What is surprising, however, is that none of his primary sources were relatives who once lived in the global village, including his mother. He did interview James Seabrook, son of Belford and grandson of C. F., and spent many tedious hours looking through microfilm of old editions of the *Bridgeton Evening News*. One of Truumees's conclusions was that "bringing over immigrants who had a strong work ethic wasn't a bad way to start a company." His essay was good enough to win awards at the local and county levels, and it was entered into a state history fair. Truumees is fluent in Estonian ("it comes in handy when you want to conduct a private conversation with an Estonian friend in a public place"), and he has traveled twice to the homeland his parents and grandparents left in haste in 1944. One of his stops was at a farm, not far from the nation's capital, that has been in his mother's family since the thirteenth century. A painting of the farm hangs in the Bridgeton home of his mother, Eevi Truumees.

Thomas Vilms, who, as a child, interviewed his grandfather, Albert, and who has heard harrowing stories from his father, Jaak, is looking forward to someday retracing the arduous and terrifying journey his grandparents and parents experienced in the mid-1940s when they escaped the Russians in Estonia, only to be forced to keep one kilometer ahead of the Red Army as it swept through eastern Europe. He hopes to travel by car, as closely as possible, the route his family traversed on foot from a point just west of Prague in Czechoslovakia to Augsberg, Germany. The displaced persons camp they were assigned to was located at the end of World War II in Augsberg in the American occupied zone. Thomas and his brother accompanied their father to Germany in 1980 when their father took a year's sabbatical from his teaching position at Colorado State University, and that visit included a tour of Augsberg. For as long as he can remember, Thomas, who is now in the software business in Washington, D.C., has an appreciation for how hard it must have been for his grandparents, both of whom were highly educated in Estonia, to work twelve hours a day in menial jobs at Seabrook Farms. "They [must have] just settled in and declared, 'Let's be the bedrock for our kids and their kids.'"

Like his brother, Andres Vilms heard about life at Seabrook Farms from his father when they were growing up in Colorado. But it wasn't until the summer of 1987, between his sophomore and junior years at Stanford University, where he was earning a bachelor's degree in history, that he decided to dig into that particular part of his family's roots. He took a job in quality control at Seabrook Brothers and Sons, the company that has resurrected the family name and is situated almost within shouting distance of the water tower that once identified Seabrook Farms. As it turned out, his immediate boss was Estonian, and not a few of the Seabrook Farms alumni from its heyday still lived in the area, including his grandfather (who later moved to Colorado to live with his son). "My job was pretty easy compared to the work my grandfather did in the early 1950s; for example, I didn't work twelve-hour shifts. It's amazing how they sacrificed to keep going in a new world." In 1999 he attended a party at the old Seabrook Community House celebrating the fiftieth anniversary of the arrival of the first Estonians at Seabrook. By then he no longer found it strange that these men and women, who had come to America homeless and penniless and then travailed many endless days and weeks, had only fond memories of those years.

When Andres Vilms went to work for Seabrook Brothers and Sons in the summer of 1987, the brothers, James M. and Charles F. II, and their five sons were celebrating their tenth anniversary as a company. James, grandson of C. F. and son of Belford, went to work for Seabrook Farms in 1958, six months before his grandfather sold the business to Seeman Brothers. Although his father and two uncles immediately resigned, he himself stayed on through the hectic years as Seeman Brothers allowed Seabrook Farms to go downhill, or perhaps gave it a not-so-gentle push over the edge, and later sold the business to Spring Mills. By the 1970s the company was called Seabrook Foods. James worked his way up to become president of the northern division, which included plants in New Jersey and several other states. One of them, of course, was the old Seabrook Farms processing plant. The CEO of Seabrook Foods at the time was Jerry Pierson, and, in 1975, he and other top company executives decided to close the original Seabrook Farms plant in Upper Deerfield, where frozen food had debuted in the 1930s. James reacted. "I was opposed to the decision, and I made a nuisance of myself, coming up with plans and projections [for saving the plant.] I continued to pursue my case until I alienated Pierson, which wasn't hard to do. Spring Mills didn't want to hear any more about [my plans,] so I quit, or I got fired. It's pretty hard to tell which it was." That was in August 1977. "I was unemployed and had no prospects, but I got to thinking if I really believed in all the projections I had made, why not go ahead and do it. My brother and I put up $100,000 and we ultimately borrowed about $20 million to build a new plant." The new plant, now twenty-five years old, is roughly three miles down the railroad track C. F. built in the 1920s to connect with the Pennsylvania-Reading Railroad out of Bridgeton. James is chairman and CEO of Seabrook Brothers and Sons, and Charles F. II is vice chairman.

The business today resembles the old Seabrook Farms in only one respect: Spinach, green beans, lima beans, and other vegetables still come in fresh from New Jersey farmers and are frozen, packed, warehoused, and sold to markets across America. The disparities between the old and new operations are striking: Seabrook Brothers and Sons owns none of the farmland; whereas the Seabrook Farms operation at its peak covered as many as three million square feet, Seabrook Brothers and Sons gets by with 450,000; fewer than 500 employees at Seabrook Brothers and Sons can now turn out a million pounds of frozen produce a year, a feat that once took thousands of workers. Technology and a new style of management have made the difference. In an interview, James Seabrook said, "We have some electronic sorters, but the other thing is a recognition that unless you put on a ton of people to sort vegetables on the conveyor belt, which is economically unsound, you can't change the raw material too much. If it comes in good, it ends up good."

When Spring Mills finally closed down operations in 1982, it turned over all the old Seabrook Farms buildings to Upper Deerfield Township in lieu of paying back taxes. Seabrook Brothers and Sons purchased the original cold storage facilities from the township, and Clement Pappas & Company, which produces cranberry and other juices, bought the processing and freezing plants. The old water tower, which still supplies the plants and what remains of the company town, including the Moore School, is still owned by the township. If James Seabrook cranes his neck just right, he can see the tower from his office window. In May 1994, thirty-five years from the day when the Old Man dealt Seabrook Farms a lethal blow, Seabrook Brothers and Sons was finally able to obtain the legal rights to the name "Seabrook Farms," and so, uncle Jack Seabrook could proudly say, "Seabrook Farms is back in the family, 101 years after A. P. and C. F. moved their farming business to the site where the old freezing plant stood."[15] Now, wherever you shop for frozen food, you probably will see, among any of the fifty brands that Seabrook Brothers and Sons packs for, the Seabrook Farms label.

We might imagine a small group of today's employees at Seabrook Brothers as they walk away from the plant at the end of the day. In the glow of the sun setting behind the woods to the west, they bid each other good-bye. If, in the growing shadows, they are then very silent, they may hear faintly from across the fields that spread north to the old water tower ghostly whispers: "Sayonora." "Paeva." "Auf Wiedersehen."

Notes

Chapter 1 Transplanting Uprooted Peoples

1. John Seabrook, "The Spinach King," *The New Yorker*, 20 and 27 February, 1995, 225.
2. John M. Seabrook, *The Henry Ford of Agriculture* (Seabrook, NJ: Seabrook Educational and Cultural Center, 1995), 2.
3. Seabrook., "The Spinach King," 225.
4. Albert Nelson Marquis, ed., *Who's Who in New Jersey* (Chicago, 1923) 128.
5. Seabrook, *The Henry Ford of Agriculture*, 7.
6. F. Alan Palmer, *This Place Called Home* (Upper Deerfield, NJ: Upper Deerfield Township Committee, 1985), 103.
7. Seabrook, *The Henry Ford of Agriculture*, 7.
8. *Ibid*.
9. *Ibid*.
10. Palmer, *This Place Called Home*, 55–56, 169.
11. *Ibid*., 105

12. Seabrook, *The Henry Ford of Agriculture*, 8.

13. Mona Gardner, "The Assembly-Line Farmer," *Reader's Digest*, January 1944.

14. Seabrook, *The Henry Ford of Agriculture*, 24–25.

15. Alfred M. Heston, *South Jersey: A History, 1664–1924*, vol. 1 (New York: Lewis Historical Publishing Company, 1924), 132.

16. *Seabrook at War*, Radio Documentary, New Jersey Historical Commission, 1995.

17. Palmer, *This Place Called Home*, 125–126.

18. Seabrook, *The Henry Ford of Agriculture*, 16.

19. Palmer, *This Place Called Home*, 124.

20. "Henry Steel Commager," in *Bill Moyers: A World of Ideas*, ed. Betty Sue Flowers (New York: Doubleday, 1989), 221–222.

21. Rei R. Noguchi, *Seabrook: A New Beginning* (Upper Deerfield: Seabrook Education and Culture Center, 1994).

22. "A Farmer with a Vision," *Bridgeton Evening News*, 22 October 1964, 4.

Chapter 2 "No Sulkers Need Apply"

1. John M. Seabrook, *The Henry Ford of Agriculture* (Seabrook, NJ: Seabrook Educational and Cultural Center, 1995), 4–5.

2. *Bridgeton Evening News*, 22 October 1964, 4.

3. Seabrook, *The Henry Ford of Agriculture*, 6.

4. *Encyclopaedia Britannica*, 15th ed., vol. 22, 171, 235.

5. Seabrook, *The Henry Ford of Agriculture*, 10–11.

6. Edward Acton, Vladimir Iu Cherniaev, and William G. Rosenberg, eds. *Critical Companion to the Russian Revolution 1914–1921* (Bloomington: Indiana University Press, 1997), 508.

7. William S. Graves, *America's Siberian Adventure* (New York: Jonathan Cape & Harrison Smith, 1931), 356.

8. F. Alan Palmer, *A Place Called Home* (Upper Deerfield, NJ: Upper Deerfield Township Committee, 1985), 104.

9. *Ibid.*

10. *Ibid.*

11. "Historic Bridgeton," *Bridgeton Evening News*, 1936, 65.

12. Alfred M. Heston, *South Jersey: A History, 1664–1924*, vol. 2 (New York: Lewis Historical Publishing Company, 1924), 941.

13. Seabrook, *The Henry Ford of Agriculture*, 11–12.

14. *Encyclopaedia Britannica*, 15th ed., vol. 29, 299.

15. Hubert G. Schmidt, *Agriculture in New Jersey* (New Brunswick: Rutgers University Press, 1973), 237.

16. Willard A. Heaps, *Wandering Workers* (New York: Crown Publishers, 1968), 14.

17. Seabrook, *The Henry Ford of Agriculture*, 17–18.

18. *Ibid.*, 18.

19. *Ibid.*, 17–18

Chapter 3 Finding a Better Way

1. William Manchester, *The Glory and the Dream: A Narrative History of America* (Boston: Little, Brown, 1973), 36.

2. John M. Seabrook, *The Henry Ford of Agriculture* (Seabrook, NJ: Seabrook Educational and Cultural Center, 1995), 18–20.

3. "Gas Balks Rioters on Jersey Farm," the *New York Times,* 10 July 1934, 1.

4. Clement Alexander Price, *Freedom Not Far Distant* (Newark: New Jersey Historical Society, 1980), 242.

5. Seabrook, *The Henry Ford of Agriculture*, 18.

6. *Seabrook at War*, Radio Documentary, New Jersey Historical Commission, 1995.

7. "Gas Balks Rioters."

8. "Wholesale Arrests Follow Rioting at Strike Scene," *Bridgeton Evening News*, 9 July 1934, 1.

9. "Agitator, Fighting Settlement, Is Rescued by Police—Prisoners Are Freed," the *New York Times*, 11 July 1934, 1.

10. "Communist Threatened with Lynching as U.S. Mediator Ends Strike," *Bridgeton Evening News*, 11 July 1934, 1.

11. "The Negro Joins the Picket Line," *Journal of Negro Life*, August 1934, 256.

12. *Negroes on the Road: A Survey of the Negro Transient in New Jersey, January–June, 1934*, State of New Jersey Emergency Relief Administration (Trenton, NJ, 1935), 24.

13. Seabrook, *The Henry Ford of Agriculture*, 20–21.

14. "Assembly-Line Farmer," *Reader's Digest*, January 1944, 96.

15. Seabrook, *The Henry Ford of Agriculture*, 25.

16. *Ibid.*, pp. 31, 32, 26.

17. *Ibid.*

18. I.C.B. Dear and M.R.D. Foot, eds., *The Oxford Companion to World War II* (Oxford: Oxford University Press, 1995), 677–679.

Chapter 4 "Let's Go to New Jersey"

1. *Oral Histories of a Community*, vol. 2, (Seabrook, NJ: Seabrook Educational and Cultural Center, 1997), 60–85.

2. "Assembly-Line Farmer," *Reader's Digest*, January 1944, 96.

3. Michi Nishiura Weglyn, *Years of Infamy: The Untold Story of America's Concentration Camps* (Seattle: University of Washington Press, 1996), 316.

4. *Ibid.*, 104–105.

5. Letter from William Huso, Relocation Officer at Gila Relocation Project in Arizona, to Margaret E. Jones, American Friends Society in Philadelphia, 8 April 1944.

6. Mitziko Sawada, "After the Camps: Seabrook Farms, New Jersey, and the Resettlement of Japanese Americans, 1944–1947," *Amerasia Journal*, 1986–1987, 117–132.

7. I.C.B. Dear and M.R.D. Foot, eds., *The Oxford Companion to World War II* (Oxford: Oxford University Press, 1995), 9.

8. Helen B. Cubberley, "I Remember When," letter dated 13 March 1994.

9. "Japanese Labor Urged to Avert Work Shortage," *Bridgeton Evening News*, 23 May 1944, 1.

10. Leonard Goodis, "The Japanese American Problem," *We Women*, April 1945, 9.

11. Weglyn, *Years of Infamy*, 60.

12. *Ibid.*, 63–65.

13. Fusaye Kazaoka, "I Remember Life in Seabrook," letter dated 22 September 1994.

14. Iddy Taniguchi Asada, "I Remember Hoover Village," letter dated 30 September 1994.

15. John Seabrook, "A Man of His Time," *The New Yorker*, 20 and 27 February 1995, 231.

Chapter 5 Beyond the Golden Door

1. *Encyclopaedia Britannica*, 15th ed., vol. 1, 847.

2. *The DP Story: The Final Report of the United States Displaced Persons Commission* (Washington: Government Printing Office, 1952), 191–193.

3. Richard W. Solberg, *Open Doors: the Story of Lutherans Resettling Refugees* (St. Louis: Concordia Publishing House, 1992), 27.

4. *Ibid.*, 37.

5. *Ibid.*, 27.

6. *Ibid.*, 37.

7. F. Alan Palmer, *This Place Called Home* (Upper Deerfield, NJ: Upper Deerfield Township Committee, 1985), 46.

8. Juhan Simonson, "The DPs are Coming!" *Global Estonian*, fall 2000, 82.

9. Palmer, *This Place Called Home*, 51.

10. "Biggest Vegetable Factory on Earth," *Life*, 3 January 1955, 41.

11. "This Is Seabrook Farms," *Quick Frozen Foods Magazine*, 1956, 3.

12. *Ibid.*, 21–22.

13. Liina Keerdoja, "I Remember Seabrook," *The Estonian Community of Seabrook, New Jersey* (Upper Deerfield: Seabrook Educational and Cultural Center, 1995), 27–28.

Chapter 6 Many Cultures, One Community

1. F. Alan Palmer, *This Place Called Home* (Upper Deerfield, NJ: Upper Deerfield Township Committee, 1985), 23–25.
2. *Ibid.*, 26.
3. *Ibid.*, 22.
4. Paul H. Noguchi, "Bean Picking at Seabrook," letter dated 25 August 1993.
5. Peeter Vilms, "I Remember Seabrook."
6. Reet Sikkemae, "I Remember Seabrook," letter dated 27 June 1996.
7. *Ibid.*
8. Ann Mariko Lowe, "Seabrook Memories," letter dated August 25, 1994.
9. "USO Presents Gala Talent Show in Seabrook Auditorium, " *The Seabrooker*, August 1945, 2.
10. Emiko Noguchi Herold, "I Remember Seabrook: The Bookmobile and Other Memories," letter dated June 1999.
11. Michi Nishiura Weglyn, *Years of Infamy* (Seattle: University of Washington Press, 1996), 268.
12. Fusaye Kazaoka, *Seabrook Village, New Jersey: Oral Histories of a Community* (Upper Deerfield, NJ: Seabrook Educational and Cultural Center, 1997).

13. Rei R. Noguchi, "Remembrances of Seabrook Village of the 1950s: A Newspaper Boy's View," letter dated 15 January 1994.

14. Ida Mueller Hintz, *Seabrook Village, New Jersey: Oral Histories of a Community* (Upper Deerfield, NJ: Seabrook Educational and Cultural Center, 1997).

15. Samah Pearson, *Seabrook Village, New Jersey: Oral Histories of a Community* (Upper Deerfield, NJ: Seabrook Educational and Cultural Center, 1994).

16. Lowe, "Seabrook Memories."

17. Harumi Taniguchi, "I Remember Life in Seabrook," letter dated 22 September 1994.

18. Hintz, *Seabrook Village*.

19. Josie Ikeda, *Seabrook Village, New Jersey: Oral Histories of a Community* (Upper Deerfield, NJ: Seabrook Educational and Cultural Center, 1994).

20. Palmer, *This Place Called Home*, 30.

Chapter 7 Reading, 'Riting and Respect

1. Elaine Glendon Laws, "I Remember Seabrook," letter dated 11 December 1999.

2. Alan Woodruff, "I Remember Seabrook School," letter dated 3 March 2000.

3. Laws, "I Remember Seabrook."

4. Alice Kinoshita, "Our Bridgeton," *We Women*, March 1946, 4.

5. *Bartlett's Familiar Quotations*, 16th ed. (Boston: Little, Brown, 1992), 564.

6. F. Alan Palmer, *This Place Called Home* (Upper Deerfield, NJ: Upper Deerfield Township Committee, 1985), 4, 155.

7. Shirley Stotz Pillow, "I Remember Seabrook," letter dated 31 January 2000.

8. Reet Sikkemae, "I Remember Seabrook.," letter dated 27 June 1996.

9. *Ibid*.

10. Rei R. Noguchi, *Seabrook: A New Beginning* (Upper Deerfield, NJ: Seabrook Educational and Cultural Center, 1994).

11. *Ibid*.

12. *Bridgeton Evening News*, 7 June 1945, 1.

13. Liina Keerdoja, "I Remember Seabrook," *The Estonian Community of Seabrook, New Jersey* (Upper Deerfield, NJ: Seabrook Educational and Cultural Center, 1995), 2 7–28.

14. *The Seabrooker*, September 1945, 2.

15. John M. Seabrook, *The Henry Ford of Agriculture* (Upper Deerfield, NJ: Seabrook Educational and Cultural Center, 1995), 40–41.

16. *Ibid*., 41–42, 44.

Chapter 8 "So Long, Seabrook"

1. "So Long, Seabrook," *Bridgeton Evening News*, 31 March 1982, 1.

2. John M. Seabrook, *The Henry Ford of Agriculture* (Upper Deerfield: Seabrook Educational and Cultural Center, 1995), 50.

3. "To All Our Employees-Growers, Suppliers and Customers," *The Seabrooker*, 27 May 1959, 3.

Notes

4. Seabrook, *The Henry Ford of Agriculture*, 52.

5. *Ibid.*, 47.

6. Seiichi Higashide, *Adios to Tears* (Honolulu: E&E Kudo, 1993), 179, 182, 183, 193.

7. *Ibid.*, 193–194, 196–198.

8. Milli Poldma, *The Estonian Community of Seabrook, New Jersey* (Upper Deerfield, NJ: Seabrook Educational and Cultural Center, 1995), 5.

9. Rei R. Noguchi, *Seabrook: A New Beginning* (Upper Deerfield, NJ: Seabrook Educational and Cultural Center, 1994).

10. Poldma, *The Estonian Community*, 25–26.

11. Donna Pearson, *Seabrook Village, New Jersey: Oral Histories of a Community* vol. 1, 1997.

12. Vallo Truumees, "I Remember Seabrook," letter dated 3 June 1996.

13. Seiki Murono, *Seabrook Village, New Jersey: Oral Histories of a Community*, vol. 1, 1997.

14. F. Alan Palmer, *This Place Called Home* (Upper Deerfield, NJ: Upper Deerfield Township Committee, 1985), 26.

15. Seabrook, *The Henry Ford of Agriculture*, 54.

Index

Index

Index

Index

Index

Index

Charles H. Harrison teaches writing at Rowan University in New Jersey and is a contributing editor for *General Store* magazine. He is also the writer and co-producer of the award-winning documentary, "Seabrook Farms Remembered." Mr. Harrison has enjoyed a long career in journalism and is the author of many books and articles on education, history, and travel.